# Eat, Sleep, Poop & Repeat

## How to Guide for Your New Baby

**Becky Brezovski**

To my daughters, Emersen & Isabella, you are my world.
To Kurtis, thank you for holding me up to reach for the stars.

**"A child must know that he is a miracle, that since the beginning of the world there hasn't been, and until the end of the world there will not be, another child like him." ~ Casals**

# Foreword

With hundreds of choices of new parenting books available at our fingertips, you may be wondering, why choose "Eat, Sleep, Poop & Repeat?" This book is a breath of fresh air. Becky does not shame or lecture the reader. Instead, it feels like she is having a conversation with you. This unpretentious parenting book is not strict and structured, but rather is written with openness and honesty, allowing the new parent to know they have time to 'get to know their baby'. The book encourages readers to educate themselves and follow their infant's cues while remembering that you, the parent to this little wonder of life, are their everything! Of utmost importance, Becky gently reminds readers to be accepting of their birth and of the postpartum recovery, in addition to the value of self-care and maintaining a loving relationship with your partner.

The clinical expertise Becky shares around birth trauma, head shape, sleep, tongue and lip ties (just to name some of what she discusses) is just the tip of her knowledge base. However, it is the basics of what every parent needs to know so they can feel confident being the greatest advocate for their child. Time is precious as a new parent and having Becky provide insight and recommendations on what professionals to seek out for certain issues, is in itself, a huge plus for every family!

As an incredible bonus, she describes with detail how to perform four techniques to help soothe and comfort your baby. The best part? Each time you pick up this book to read from cover to cover again, to peruse a certain chapter to help you find an answer, or to reassure yourself that you are doing something right as a new parent – a nugget of knowledge that didn't register previously or a powerful idea of something to try will

spring out at you! Keep this book within arm's reach so you are able to refer back to it again and again. I had the honour of working with Becky for nine years; consulting with her and co-managing treatment plans for our littlest patients. Becky and I are strong advocates for individuals to create a multi-faceted healthcare and wellness team that is able to support the individual and offer alternatives.

Becky is a wealth of knowledge, has tremendous insight, and is willing to teach and share her experiences. She works with multiple different disciplines to find the right answer for each individual child. Her desire to continue to learn, explore, study, and master her skill is unmatched. I am already waiting for her next book!

-   Dr. April Ruzycki, D.C.


A labor of love, this book is a great balance of knowledge, science and experience. Becky brings her 20 years of practice as a CranioSacral Therapist to the homes of those who are searching for a gentle, hands on approach for understanding and connecting with their newborn.

Her honesty and candid discussions range from newborn cues, postpartum mood changes in parents to recovery from both birth trauma and delivery. She provides a framework that normalizes the often terrifying world of bringing home a newborn. What stood out to me the most about Becky's book is her regular reminders that we need to take care of ourselves as well as our baby. She shines a light on the important topics such as postpartum depression and healing in both parents. This is often forgotten both in the doctor's office and with our families once these sweet babies join our homes!

With her tips, tricks and honesty, this book will leave you confident and reassured that you are not alone on this wild journey into parenthood! I am thrilled that she is sharing her knowledge with all of you so that you also can benefit from her gifts. I can attest first hand that her tips and tricks work as my babes and I have benefited from her support. I hope you and your little one do as well.

- Dr. Kristine Woodley M.D.

# DISCLAIMER

The information contained within this book is not intended or implied to be a substitute for professional medical advice, diagnosis, or treatment. Please always seek advice from a medical professional.

# Table of Contents

# Introduction

Congratulations, it's a baby! If you have ever been blessed with the moment of becoming a parent, you've heard this sentence. Whether you've been handed your beautiful bundle through adoption, surrogacy, or mother nature herself; this moment is both unforgettable and terrifying.

You convince yourself that you are prepared. Car seat, blankets, and gadgets that took you longer to assemble than your Ikea table. Then the moment comes, baby in arms, and they just let you leave. Typically, you are handed a few pamphlets on colic or vitamins, they check your car seat, and off you go into the wild. That is exactly how it feels. Typically, you have your partner drive no more than 1.5 kilometers per hour all the way home. If you had it your way, you would have a police escort, and the streets would be cleared. You hold your breath the entire way because, well, my gosh, you are now responsible for this brand new life. I would like to reassure you that this feeling goes away, but alas, this is parenthood.

Instincts are supposed to kick in during your extreme exhaustion, so at the minimum, this precious bundle will have food and shelter. But wait, what if you can't get them to eat? No worries, a quick trip to the doctors should clear all that up, right? Placing your vulnerable baby on that cold scale, measuring, poking, and examining just to be told they are doing great. This whirlwind takes all of three minutes, but what about all of your questions? It's fine, there are books and the internet for that, right?

So, as the baby sleeps soundly on you, you spiral through the wormhole of baby information on the web. Within minutes, you are convinced you have no idea what position they should sleep, what color their poop should be, or what age they should move out. You now do not even know how many times they should eat, what they should eat, or what you should eat. All the books begin to sound the same, and most are written by doctors. Who are you supposed to trust?

Now I want you to put all those books down. Ask someone to watch that precious human for thirty minutes and have a relaxing shower. I want to introduce you to a real, honest, and practical book. One not written by doctors, but by a woman who has been treating, healing, and "baby whispering" her way through life for over twenty years. A woman who hears you, cares, and wants this journey to be healthy, happy, and memorable.

I am so confident you will love this book that by the time you are through, this will be the gift you give to all your special people about to become parents too. Once you have some time under your belt as a parent, and refer back to this book on multiple occasions, you will feel empowered and have trust in you. That is what is most important—creating a loving, trusting bond within families. Now, let's talk about sleep, feeding, and, of course, poop!

# Chapter 1:

# You Have a New Baby, the

# First Days!

*Congrats on your new job title. Hope the baby boss takes it easy on you.*—Kristin McCarthy

You did it! You grew your family by one—or more if you were blessed with multiples—I will pray for you. Whether through adoption, surrogacy, or birth, you gained the title of *parent*, and life is about to change. It will feel like chaos for this first bit, but finding the right resources will help you feel more in control. Let's look at some ways that may make this journey a bit easier on you and the rest of the family.

## Learning Your Baby's Cues

Have you ever been in a social situation and read the room wrong? Maybe it was a work event, or you were meeting your future in-laws for the first time. After scanning the room, you felt that most people were laughing, enjoying themselves, and most were relaxed. What a great time for a joke, right? As the words are falling from your mouth, you begin to notice cues. "Sally" is placing her hands across her mouth. "James" is looking at you wide-eyed in total disbelief. Your boss has left the room entirely.

While my brain gathers these cues, it begins to tally the social disaster I just created. Why didn't I stop the joke when the cues started? Some of us are great at picking up on cues, but there are a few of us who could use a refresher course.

That being said, how many of you know the cues that your new baby is trying to get you to see? Well, before your wee human can speak, there will be times that frustration will set in and you will hear yourself say, "Why can't you just tell me what is wrong with you, what do you need from me?"

Your baby's body language can tell you a great deal about how they are feeling, what is bothering them, what they need, and, of course, how you can help them. By educating yourself on these cues and responding to them, you will build a solid, trusting relationship with your baby. This is only going to enhance and strengthen their development going forward.

Every baby will give cues, but each baby will also develop their own cue "language" as well. Be patient with yourself; trust that in no time you will know and understand these cues better than anyone. Below you will find some specific cues indicative of babies' needs.

## *Baby Cues Indicating "I Am Hungry"*

Here are some cues to watch for in your wee human, indicating they may be hungry. If they are a newborn, you will want to watch for these cues every one to two hours. As they get to be about four to six months old, you can look for them every three to four hours.

- turns head towards the breast, regardless of who is holding them
- baby sucking on their fist
- puckers, smacks, or licking of the lips

## *Baby Cues Indicating "I Am Tired"*

Nothing makes a new parent more delighted than a content, sleepy baby. But missing those sleepy-time cues can leave us with an over-tired, fussy wee one. So, what should we be on the lookout for?

- Baby is just staring off into space, much like we do when we are tired.
- Great big yawns and stretches from the wee one.

- Ear or hair pulling; oftentimes we confuse this with teething, but in newborns they are sleepy.
- Rubbing those teeny little eyes because they are sleepy.
- Crying, yes they will let out small little cries letting you know they need a nap.
- Losing interest in play because they are getting tired.

## *Baby Cues Indicating "I Am Over It"*

Babies are much like us in the sense that they too can become overwhelmed by visitors, toys, sounds, or light. It is important to watch for cues and know when they have just had enough.

- The baby will be squirming or trying to push away from you.
- Watch for them trying to cover their tiny, little faces.
- You will see them turn their head away from the light or noise.
- Excessive crying and louder than normal.
- Baby will kick and wave arms erratically.

## *Baby Cues Indicating I Want to Play*

So, how exactly do we know when our new baby wants to play? They are so tiny and fragile; do they have the capacity to tell us? They most certainly do. Below you will find the cues indicating play.

- They make direct eye contact with you.
- Beautiful moments when they reach their tiny arms out to you.
- Big smiles appear on their faces when making eye contact.
- Bright, wide-open eyes and smooth movements.
- They make cooing and babbling noises.

Now that you are equipped with a library of baby cues, let's explore some wonderful tips and tricks to make your parenting journey a pleasant one.

# Conscious Parenting

Let's be honest for a moment here. From the second we find out that we are going to be parents, what do we do? After the initial panic, we start to educate ourselves. Books on parenting, podcasts on parenting, and social media groups for parenting. You have lengthy discussions with your partner about how this is all going to go down. Bold statements about how you will never feed your children sugar, and how you are parenting the complete opposite way your parents did. One rule or parenting strategy after another. Then, one day, the baby arrives and we begin implementing all of our well-researched tools. Three days in and we cannot understand why nothing is working. What you failed to realize is that these children come into this world with their own unique personalities. The one size fits all parenting styles of the past tried conforming all of us to the same style, even though we are all different. Now is the time to get to know your baby—only then will you know how to be the best parent.

## *The Power of Positive Touch*

Also known as infant massage, this can be a positive and healthy way to get to know your baby. You should consider this a form of communication between you and your wee human. For months, touch is one of the few ways babies communicate, so soothingly placing your hands on them will create many benefits. Remember to keep an eye on those cues. You want to engage in touch when the baby is content, happy, and fed. As well, you want to keep an eye on the baby for cues to tell you when it is time to stop. You want to watch for the following.

- baby arching their back
- trying to crawl or walk away
- they are falling asleep
- excessive crying
- tightly closed fists
- rapid limb movement

Now that we know the baby is ready, able, and willing, how do we begin? Follow these step-by-step instructions for a happy and relaxed baby in no time.

### *Opening Stroke*

This prepares your wee one's body for the positive touch that is going to begin. There is no need to undress your baby to do this stroke. Most babies feel more content when covered, so use your discretion. Place your flat, open, and warm hands on the top of your baby's head or tummy. Very gently, slowly move down both sides of the body from the head to the toes. This gentle touch alone can increase a baby's cardiac and respiratory health. It can improve their sleep quality as well as enhance their neurodevelopment.

## *Tummy Strokes*

Utilizing this stroke can help to relieve symptoms of colic, constipation, and improves digestion. It is also fantastic at relaxing the stomach area. You must always complete this in a clockwise motion. Draw a wide circle around your baby's belly button with the palm of your hand. Feel free to repeat this move as often as you and the baby are enjoying it.

## *Foot Massage*

There is nothing like a good foot massage to also help and relieve pretty much any issue your little wee might be having. From gas pain to teething pain, a gentle foot rub can be the solution.

1. Head and Teeth: toes and the middle of each toe touches the sinuses.
2. Chest: the toe mounds to the toe arch.
3. Upper Abdomen: the arch of the toes or about a fingers width down from the toes.
4. Lower Abdomen: the thumb space above the heel.

5. Pelvis: the heel.

## *Face Massage*

Use a simple stroke technique by using your thumb. Begin by moving across the cheekbones with a feather light stroke, follow that by sweeping your thumb under the cheekbones from the lip line out to the ears. Next, lightly sweep up between the eyes to the middle of the forehead. From here, gently stroke from the middle of the forehead using both thumbs out towards the ears. Lastly, from ears down the side of the face to the neck to drain. Repeat it several times, as long as your little wee is tolerating it and not showing you any cues that they may be overstimulated. Remember to move in one direction, away from the center, and not back the way you came to prevent backflow of lymphatic fluid. This little routine offers 5 basic health benefits as follows:

1. Helps with colds and congestion.
2. Promotes relaxation for a good night's sleep.
3. Helps with teething pain.
4. Helps with ear infections.
5. Releases oxytocin and decreases cortisol (stress hormone).

## *After Your Positive Touch Time*

When your positive touch time has ended, there are some important things to remember. After applying these massage-type touches, there is a good chance your baby may want to feed. There has been a decent amount of stimulation, and this naturally increases their thirst. It may be nice to end with a nice warm bath. Then, wrap them up in a warm, fluffy towel, followed by lots of cuddles.

Keep an eye on the sleepy cues, and once you notice the baby is tired, lay them down and allow time to rest.

### Kangaroo Care

While we are discussing positive touch, let's not forget how important it is for the baby to feel you skin-to-skin. Any parent shouldn't hesitate to remove their shirt and place the baby, wearing nothing more than a diaper, against their chest. You will typically notice the wee one settles quickly. The benefits of this are incredible.

1. Regulates the body temperature of the wee human.
2. Can help increase the baby's weight.
3. Improve their oxygen saturation levels.
4. Offers your new wee one pure, blissful, relaxation.
5. Helps to regulate their heartbeat.
6. Last, who doesn't love cuddles?

# Pacifiers

When babies suffer from oral tension, feeding issues, tongue tie, high palate, were delivered via vacuum, nursed, or bottle fed, the choice of a pacifier should come down to one important question. What is baby's tongue doing?

A tongue that rests on the top of the mouth is optimal. Why? Because tongue position in the mouth is not just about the tongue but plays a wider role in several body functions. Such as swallowing, breathing, speaking, chewing, lower limb muscle strength, posture and oral health. The inability of the tongue resting on the roof of the mouth can cause open mouth breathing, increased neck pain, jaw pain, sleep apnea, problems with vision, and dental cavities. Furthermore, when the tongue rests on the floor of the mouth, over several years, permanent changes set in with face shape and chin position.

Opinions of when to start a pacifier vary depending on who you talk to, but I'll tell you right now that you can start whenever you're ready. There is no clinical evidence that waiting 4-6 weeks makes a difference to the success of feeding by introducing a pacifier. (O'Connor et al. 2009).

With so many options on the market how do you know if the one you've picked is right for your baby? Pacifiers have different shapes and stamps of approval by clinicians, dentists, lactation consultants and occupational therapists. Pacifiers are marketed as glow-in-the-dark, have air holes to allow for breathability, curbed, shield skin from irritation, textured silicone, a high percentage of "nipple acceptance", while others are coloured to coordinate with outfits.

However, it's the design that goes into the mouth that should matter the most. I have 5 categories for pacifiers for infants 0-6 months:

*"The Nipple"*

The nipple option is longer, thin, and mimics the correct position of the tongue for nursing as it lands on the tongue. These are by far my most preferable choice as it allows the tongue to cup, pull, and rest in a position that doesn't add stress to the hard palate. Often, they have a space to allow a finger to go through it. I like to recommend this option for easy access to monitor your baby's tongue position while sucking.

### "The Gem Shape"

There is a silicone, gem shaped pacifier on the market that is truly impressive. The design allows the lips to relax, bring the tongue forward, and jaw movement can occur with its flare shield design. Developed with a pediatric dentist, this design is a game changer.

### "The Orthodontic"

The orthodontic pacifier has a semi round top, flat bottom and thin neck, this shape allows the pacifier to press broadly into the roof of the mouth, and to sit on the tongue which allows the tongue to suck and rest. This mimics the natural movement of the muscles of the mouth.

### "The Column" - The Original Orthodontic Shape

The Column pacifier has a broad shaped nipple, a thick neck and a smooth symmetrical shape. Often they are small size and often marketed for preemies. These do not encourage the tongue to grip and drag, or take the tongue to the roof of the mouth. If your baby has oral tendencies like biting, chomping, or has a hard time nursing, this type of pacifier is not a great fit for you. Your baby might do better with a longer nipple, or the gem shaped pacifier, to rest on the tongue and to encourage muscle movement versus "chomping".

*"The Bubble"*

The bubble showcases a round ball as the tip. They are made of natural rubber or BPA free silicone. These are my least favorite option as it presses into the soft space of the hard palate. A problematic example would be having a "High Arch Palate." The vault of the mouth is high and narrow. Using a bubble pacifier does not allow the hard palate to come down as it is continually pressed upon. In an ideal situation, the baby would be seeing a practitioner who does oral work in conjunction with providing home exercises. Using this type of pacifier can exacerbate the problem rather than soothe your little one.

# Baby Gadget Overload

Have you been to a baby store lately? Invited to a baby shower and become overwhelmed by the gadgets? Gone are the days of simple, and I believe we are doing ourselves and our children a disservice.

In today's baby gadget market, you will find an item to keep your baby entertained or as they call it, "stimulated" for days—swooshing chairs, swings with USB chargers, strollers with GPS tracking, and cribs that origami into treehouses. I am all about making life a bit easier, but when I visit a new parent's home and the baby is never being held, it is a cause for concern.

Actual "activity" stations are set up throughout. Once the wee one is fed, the marathon begins. First, the Megatron

3000 bouncy chair is guaranteed to have your baby ready for the Olympics in no time. The second the baby makes a fuss, they are catapulted to the next station. What do we have here? The Whisper 750 Swing-o-Matic, let us lull your baby to sleep as you sit back and relax.

Don't get me wrong, all parents have the right to relax, and parent as they see fit. I just want it to be known that a pattern is emerging of wee humans not getting enough physical, human touch, and we should be concerned. The amount of time they spend laying on their backs or propped up in these chairs plays into their motor and physical development. Their muscle strength and motor skills will be affected.

What could be done better? We just need to get back to basics. Clear out the gadgets and allow your littles to roam on the floor. Spend as much time as you can holding your new bundle, even while vacuuming. The feel and warmth they experience while traveling with you cannot be achieved through any gadget. Get outdoors and allow them to become visually stimulated as well. No need to stress about all of those expensive gadgets. In those first few months, you are all that tiny human needs.

## Visitors Need Boundaries

We all know the excitement and anticipation that comes along with bringing a new baby home. All of your friends and family have followed the progress of your pregnancy, adoption, or surrogacy. Now, the bundle has arrived and they all want their turn to visit, hold, bounce, swaddle, and coo over them. But what is best for you and the tiny one? This is the perfect time to discuss the boundaries that you will need to implement in regards to visitors.

Of course, you want to share in the joy, but your first responsibility is to yourself and that new baby. Putting those needs first should never come with a guilt-trip. Anyone who tries to hand one of those to you needn't bother. Here is a simple list of rules to help with those first few weeks. Do not be afraid to inform your guests of this list prior to their visit. If they can't support this and respect your boundaries, they can wait and visit once the baby is older.

- Don't expect to hold the baby during this first visit.
- Stay away if you are sick.
- No kissing baby on the face or hands—your germs transmit to their hands and we all know babies always put their hands in their mouth. Let's do our best to keep those germs away.
- Please wash your hands first.
- We appreciate it if you would avoid strong perfumes.
- No posting photos without permission. It doesn't matter if you are the grandparent, godparent, auntie, or Lady GaGa herself, if you did not grow said tiny human, adopt or gain guardianship of, then I repeat—DO NOT POST! "But the parent has pictures all over social media, what's the difference?" I control who sees my posts, I cannot control who sees yours. DO NOT POST!
- Give our crying baby back to the parents.

- We appreciate no unsolicited advice.
- Ask first, don't just show up. We may be napping.
- We love short visits; it allows us to keep baby on schedule.
- Keep noise to a minimum, baby may be napping.

Sticking to these boundaries will ensure that your new family will settle in with the least amount of anxiety, stress, and distractions. This is the time to explore and enjoy each other.

You may be reading this and thinking to yourself, "That's all fine and good, but are you going to tell my parents they can't come to visit their new grandbaby right away?" Having a child means having tough conversations. Let's start with the grandparents because they will have plenty of opinions on raising their grandchild. Generally speaking, grandparents mean well. Oftentimes, they will not understand your way of parenting. Your choices for nutrition, clothing, or even what name you choose can be up for debate because that is, "Not how we did that in our day."

We want to foster a positive relationship with our parents and have a solid foundation for our children and their grandparents. How do we manage this? Boundaries, set them, and do it now. Immediately following this, you need to have a conversation. Be sure that the grandparents, aunts, uncles, or whomever understand why these are in place. It is not uncommon for people to think boundaries were made to keep them away. Alleviate any fears of this kind. Remind these loved ones that you want to foster a healthy relationship between them and your baby. Don't be afraid to remind them what a great job they did with you as a parent, and now you need the space to emulate that. You can appreciate their advice, but you feel disrespected if they don't trust you to parent your way. Lastly, tell them that this is their time to relax and enjoy the fun stuff. You parent and they can play!

# Newborns in a Post Covid World

Up until this point, we have stressed the importance of babies being held and nurtured. How skin-to-skin contact has almost a dozen health benefits. But what about the babies born during the pandemic? All of these adorable wee humans born after March 2020, came into this world already facing adversity.

Depending on where you, your surrogate, or adoptive mother gave birth, it was not a typical, peaceful experience. Hospital rooms were a terrifying sight. Staff were adorned in personal protective equipment consisting of face shields, eye protections, gloves, and so on. The birthing patient also was seen wearing masks, and little skin to be seen anywhere.

Some provinces, states, and countries wouldn't even allow a partner or support person in the room when the baby was born. It was a sterile, frightening, and lonely experience for the birthing participant. How did this affect all those babies?

According to Statistics Canada, the first year of the pandemic alone saw the birth of 358, 604 babies nationwide. Studies are already being conducted on these precious beings, and the results are not great. These tiny brains are complex, but what we do know is that it is of the utmost importance for them to get plenty of exposure and stimulation because that is how the neural pathways develop. It is these pathways that—as these babies grow and mature—regulate their language, cognition, and emotion. These early studies are showing that the babies who were born into isolation during the pandemic have had an impact on their early development. There has also been an increase in delayed language and motor skills (Aziz, 2022).

Highly acclaimed researchers from Columbia University studied 255 wee ones born between March and December 2020. They discovered significantly lower scores on fine motor and gross motor skills compared to babies born pre-pandemic.

So, what does this all mean? Specialists and pediatricians are recommending that babies born during the pandemic be closely monitored for any red flags in development. Another issue that has come up is that many of these babies haven't had regular check-ups because the pandemic has forced us inside and virtual appointments. A good start would be to begin scheduling regular check-ins with your healthcare team.

In summary, the pandemic years have taken an extensive toll on this universe and everyone in it. Anyone who decided to add to their family during Covid-19 missed out on the close family bond that goes along with it. No baby showers or baptisms. Many missed ultrasounds and had solo births. It was a lonely and isolated event. Now, we need to take time to heal. Luckily, our wee ones brains' are elastic. If we are proactive and intervene now, we can heal their brains, too. First step is an evaluation, followed by patience, love, and a path of growth and healing.

# Chapter 2:

# Birth Trauma

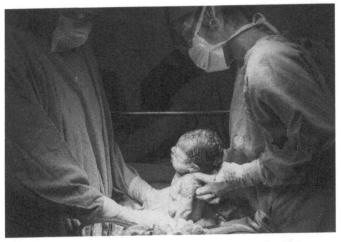

*We don't just leave our feelings about our birth at the hospital.—*
Melissa J. Bruijn

Is there one specific thing that you could think of right now that we all have in common? Okay, yes it is true, we all poop. More on that fascinating topic later. What I was actually alluding to is the fact that regardless of where we live, how old we are, or what language we speak, we have all been born.

The one piece of that puzzle that sets us apart is the actual birthing experience. From water births to cesarean sections, our journey into this world makes us unique. I feel we need to take a moment to discuss and educate important details surrounding birth trauma.

Those last few weeks before the arrival of the baby are a lot. We begin to question absolutely everything. Do we have enough diapers, do we even *have* diapers? Some will choose to formulate a birth plan and some will try to go with the flow. Either way, as the delivery date gets closer, anxiety kicks in. It all boils down to us attempting to maintain control out of a situation that can become out of control quickly.

When referring to birth trauma, it does not have to be catastrophic. Let's break this down into a few different scenarios. The following stories were created for effect and the people are not real.

## Birth Plan Nightmares

Meet Lucy and her husband Tom. They anxiously arrived at the hospital today to deliver their first baby. Lucy has been laboring at home most of the night, and after a cervical check, she appears to be seven centimeters dilated. Her birth plan states no medical intervention. She wants this birth to be as natural as possible. After about 45-minutes, Lucy has underestimated her pain tolerance and has asked for an epidural. By the time they can retrieve this for her, the baby has other plans.

Within one hour of her arrival, she is fully dilated and she is being instructed to push. Her family has filled the waiting room, anxiously awaiting the arrival of the baby.

Time stands still and after three hours of pushing the doctors decide for Lucy that she needs forceps. She is screaming in agony and her husband is terrified. After that fails, they then decide to attach a vacuum to the baby's head to help with extraction. Tom, the baby's father, is horrified and asking questions, but is told to remain calm and all of this is perfectly normal. They need to get the baby out. Lucy is exhausted, sobbing, and no longer has the energy to advocate for herself. Her husband tries to explain this isn't what they wanted. This controlled chaos ensues for what seems like hours. 20-minutes later, a bruised and startled baby is taken immediately to the Neonatal Intensive Care Unit (NICU).

Mom is shaken, exhausted, and terrified, and dad has left with the baby. Within three days this family leaves the hospital with their new daughter. Once they arrive home, Lucy sobs while she holds her new baby close. She keeps repeating how sorry she is, that she wanted to protect her. She is terrified she will hurt her. Tom, the new dad, cannot sleep and spends countless hours through the night researching ways to help his wife and baby. They are both stunned the hospital had no advice when they left. This young family will be left in this hyper, anxious state for months. Outside family and friends will chalk it up to them being overly paranoid and too cautious. This is not the case at all.

This couple went in with an expectation of receiving respect and care. What they ended up with was Lucy's body being man-handled and manipulated with no explanations or options given. This was disrespectful and traumatic at best. Baby was then whisked off, gone were those visions of mom holding her close. So, what are the repercussions for the baby?

Anatomically, babies are built to handle pressure during delivery. A slow, rhythmic delivery is the perfect opportunity for the 13 cranial bones in the baby's skull to squeeze, overlap, and move over the membrane of the skull. But when force has been added to the cranium to help assist in delivery, trauma can happen, creating tension in the membrane and shifting in bone alignments. If a vacuum is used, it can create a pull from the hard palate, which can create sucking and feeding issues, torticollis, and create restriction within the baby's nervous system, cranial nerves, musculoskeletal system, and gastrointestinal system.

When Lucy and Tom left the hospital that day, their newborn was checked out from head to toe. A quick check in the mouth, under the tongue, and no issues were found. Or were they missed? In most cases, tension won't show up until days, or even weeks after discharge.

Educating yourself on the signs to watch for is the best way to support you and your newborn. Even better, gathering yourself an amazing healthcare team prior to birth, will have you feeling supported and empowered. If Lucy and Tom had an educated team behind them, they would have had advocates in a time of chaos. Explanations and answers would have been available. This is imperative in times when parents are in a traumatic state and are going through the motions as directed by physicians and nurses. Gathering that team, interviewing and visiting them to get a sense of what they offer, will have you equipped to better handle these situations. Then, after the baby is born, you have them on board to examine the baby as issues arise with feedings, poop, sleep, and so on.

## Welcome Home Wee One

Our next couple, Josh and Michael, had waited almost ten years to become parents. The nursery—decorated with zoo animals—had been ready for two years. After three adoptions had fallen through, they decided on a surrogate. Baby was due any day and the excitement was boiling over.

The blinking clock read 3:28 a.m. and they couldn't get to her home quick enough. A home birth surrounded by calm, relaxing music and her doula by her side. No solid birth plan, just do what the baby needs, and stay home as long as possible. The Papas were available for anything their surrogate needed. Every single person agreed that things were going beautifully. There was singing, laughter, dimmed lights, and scents of lavender and vanilla floated through the air.

Almost 24 hours into labor, discussions started to take place. How long should we be doing this before medical intervention? Then, her water broke and it was agreed that it would only be safe to continue for 12 more hours at home. The doula was fantastic with her bag of tricks, attempting to get things moving. Within the next hour, the baby's heartbeat dropped significantly with each contraction. An ambulance was called as it was determined the cord was around the neck.

Immediately, the mood in the room changed. As much as the doula tried to maintain her calm voice, it was evident this was serious. Once at the hospital, it was like we no longer had a choice. The surrogate was rushed into surgery and not too long after, a nurse appeared to tell both dad's they could see their new son in the NICU.

In complete disbelief, they followed the nurse until their eyes fell upon their tiny son. Tubes, wires, and loud beeps consumed their senses. It would be weeks of tube feeds and blood work before he would be strong enough to come home. Their surrogate physically recovered well and would take time to recover emotionally. But what about the baby; how did this birthing trauma affect him?

Historically, women are known for discussing their labor and delivery stories. Tales of long labors and painful recoveries are a common theme. The one thing you don't tend to hear are conversations surrounding how the babies handled the stress of those same deliveries. To be fair, if any of the wee ones spent time in the NICU, parents often recall the terrifying nights hovering over them. They make mentions of their birth weights, all the wires attached to their baby's tiny body, but again, no mention of the overall impact.

Let's break this down. For generations, our doctors and nurses have been telling us that babies don't have the capacity to have emotion or feel pain. If they needed to come and take your baby from you for a "small" procedure, you were "not to worry" because your precious bundle wouldn't even remember a thing. For generations, North American newborn males have been subjected to circumcisions for a myriad of reasons. Once again, your brand new baby is whisked off and you are told there is no need to worry. "He won't feel a thing, just give him a few extra snuggles when we return." These sweet wee ones are then restrained and surgery is performed without regard for their pain, or basic human rights. Whether it is a lengthy delivery, or a traumatic one that ends with weeks in the NICU, the only direction parents are given is to give lots of extra love and cuddles.

There may be discussion about physical delays to keep an eye out for, but where is the conversation about everything else this baby just endured?

# What Your Baby Remembers

Research into the brain of babies has exploded over the last 50 years. Mid-century, you could count approximately 500 research papers world-wide regarding this topic. Today, we are well over 2000 books and papers and growing. But what have we learned?

Most of what scientists and doctors believed they knew, was wrong. After constant testing, it was determined that babies are always learning, observing, and picking up on things; they learn from their environment, exactly like we do. More exciting than that, is the discovery that babies know more than we expected them to know, and at an earlier age, even in the womb.

With today's technology we are able to track babies inside the womb better than ever. With the assistance of fiber optics, electron microscopes, ultrasounds, and a few high tech measuring tools, scientists have been able to plot an entire developmental scale of the nervous system. In particular, studies show that the sense of hearing develops around 20 weeks gestation and at eight weeks, by stroking the cheek with a hair, a reaction shows us that tactile sensitivity is developed (Chamberlain, 1988/1998).

With such rapid advancements in science and technology, coupled with an interest in exploring the brains and development of babies in the womb, we are uncovering fascinating things. Now let's ask ourselves these questions. If we now know that babies' senses and motor skills are developing in the womb, and their brains are capable of reacting, responding, and thinking by the time they are born, then why would they not remember their births? Why would they not have a response to pain? Why wouldn't they be traumatized by a 36 hour labor, followed by a forceps delivery? My goodness, why would they not be overly stimulated laying in an incubator after laying in mom's womb?

It would be preposterous to then assume babies wouldn't have trauma from complicated births. We bring our new bundles home and oftentimes are met with a fussy baby who won't sleep, latch, or settle. Immediately doctors or well meaning family members shower us with advice. We are told everything from, you are holding the baby too much, to the baby having gas, to the baby is just sensing your anxiety.

In fact, this sweet, tiny human is suffering from the effects of birth trauma. Let's have a look at what some of those can include.

- Tongue issues: Tension in the muscles of every muscle group affects the tongue! This can occur during an excessively long vaginal delivery, forceps or vacuum birth. If we have tension from birth, we will see issues from tongue mobility, sucking, swallowing, speech problems, torticollis, plagiocephaly, reflux, digestion, and constipation.
- In these same instances, when extra tension is placed on the muscles for an extended amount of

time during birth, you can also see occasions of sacral imbalances, scoliosis, and, at times, delayed gross and fine motor skills. There have been some reported cases of sensor processing concerns as well.

- Mentioned earlier, the force added to the baby and their delicate 13 cranial bones (that will eventually fuse into eight) are designed to squeeze, overlap, and move over the membrane of the skull. But when force has been added to the cranium to help assist in delivery, trauma can happen creating tension in the membrane and shifting in bone alignments. A vacuum during birth can create a pull from the hard palate which can create sucking, feeding issues, torticollis, and create restriction within the baby's nervous system, cranial nerves, musculoskeletal system, and gastrointestinal system.

It is understandable that reading these words will raise fears and concerns in any parent who had a traumatic birth. There is good news, and solid ways to help heal both the baby and you after all you have both endured.

## How to Heal

Fast forward to the new wee one safe at home, and you are now educated on what the side-effects are of the birth trauma you both went through. Let's equip you with the tools you need to heal and move forward with your family.

To begin, understand that this new precious baby is quick to forgive. Your first step in the process of helping both you and your baby is forgiving yourself. Nothing you did created the situation for your baby. You are both home and safe. Feel that, and embrace it.

Next, I want you to find a calm, relaxing space in your home. Pick a time when the baby is also calm, maybe right after a feeding. Swaddle them and hold them close. It would be ideal if you could make eye contact, and have some skin-to-skin contact as well. In a soothing, soft, voice I want you to talk to your wee one about the entire experience. How you wanted it to go, what was out of your control, and how you will keep them safe. Let them hear your voice, reassure them they are safe, and allow yourself to take back the control you lost. This will be so healing for you both. This may bring that connection together for you that you didn't get in the hospital if the baby was in the NICU. It may be that intimate moment you didn't get because you needed immediate medical attention. Enjoy the calm, the quiet, and each other.

## Postpartum Recovery

To cover postpartum recovery, I would like to focus on our two birthing stories above. Let's discuss how to support Lucy's postpartum, our traumatic hospital birth; and that of Josh and Michael, our couple who's surrogate delivered and baby landed in the NICU.

Lucy headed home and was met with a house filled with people. Her in-laws decided it would be lovely to throw her a coming home party, just shy of 50 people and food for days. As Lucy shuffled through the foyer, she burst into tears. The guests all believed she was overwhelmed with their generosity, but that couldn't be further from the truth.

Breast milk had leaked through her shirt and was running down her unrecognizable stomach. She was convinced her episiotomy stitches were stuck to her maxi pad, which felt like a mattress between her legs. Her hair hadn't been washed in four days, she couldn't decipher if her breath smelled worse than her body and she hadn't pooped in a week. Was that her boss sitting on her couch holding a freaking gift? Enter level ten melt down.

She did not leave her bedroom for the next 12 days. Her sister gave her sponge baths, fed her some soup, and convinced her to talk to someone. By someone, she meant a professional…it was time.

Postpartum depression (PPD) is defined as a mood disorder involving intense psychological depression that typically occurs within one month after giving birth, lasts more than two weeks, and is accompanied by other symptoms, such as social withdrawal, difficulty bonding with baby, or feelings of guilt (*Merriam-Webster Dictionary*, 2022).

It is very common for a new mom to experience brief moments of "baby blues" after arriving home. These feelings can range from difficulty sleeping to bouts of crying. The difference is, they don't last long and you generally feel like you have a handle on it. PPD is far more severe and long-lasting. Always keep in mind that this is not a flaw, but usually a side-effect of birth trauma. Here is a list of PPD symptoms.

- restlessness
- panic attacks
- anxiety attacks
- intense irritability
- anger outburst
- chronic fatigue
- no longer interested in things you once enjoyed
- insomnia
- excessive crying
- depression
- severe mood swings
- withdrawing from friends and family
- loss of appetite
- not wanting to bond with baby
- fear of failure as a mother
- thoughts of harming baby
- thoughts of harming yourself
- thoughts of death or suicide

If you are feeling any of these listed above, know you are not alone and please reach out. All branches of medical, holistic, psychological, and nutritional fields offer ways to combat and relieve PPD. You do not have to feel shame or guilt alone.

Do you remember Josh and Michael? They couldn't wait to become parents and enlisted the help of a surrogate to make that possible. The delivery was going beautifully, but before too long, circumstances dictated an ambulance ride to the hospital. The first glimpse of their new son was in the NICU.

Weeks would go by before they were able to take him home. What a joyous occasion it was when they did. They had planned for his day home to be a quiet home-coming with just the three of them. Lights were low, no visitors and they spent time reconnecting with their son. Within days, Josh noticed a significant change in Michael. He was staying awake all night and obsessively cleaning the house. When asked about it, Michael simply stated that he was protecting their son from germs. When visitors started coming over, Michael would limit them to ten minutes of holding the baby. They had to use hand sanitizer, and wear a mask. He said he had read studies about how weak a baby's immune system is and he was protecting their son. He started having all of their groceries delivered, stating the less they entered a building filled with people, the less chance of bringing germs inside. He didn't want to take their son to the park, or anywhere public that posed a risk in his eyes. Michael's behavior was becoming a problem. It was affecting his life, as well as the rest of the family. It was time to talk to someone.

## *Postpartum Recovery in Spouses*

What we are witnessing with Michael is very common. When one spouse kicks in taking care of the basic duties of the baby, diapering, feeding, and so on, the other may begin to spiral into protection mode. We see this most often when a birth trauma has occurred. Before the birth, everything made sense. There was a plan, the baby would be born and then protected for life. When that plan shifts and either parent feels they couldn't protect the baby during the chaos, that is terrifying. Once the baby is finally home, that same parent now vows to protect fiercely, for life.

This can look like obsessively disinfecting, baby proofing overload, triple checking car seats, installing house alarms, insisting visitors disinfect themselves, and even staying up all night keeping watch over the baby.

This behavior isn't healthy and Michael is wearing himself out. He isn't aware that by doing this, he won't be any good in supporting Josh or his new son. PPD in spouses looks just like it does in moms. The same symptoms listed above apply. It may appear differently in them at times, but they are not exempt.

Michael needs to take some time with his new son. Hold him skin-to-skin, looking him in the eye, and explain what happened. Tell him why he couldn't be there when he was born but assure him that he can depend on you now. Hold him close while you tell him all the amazing things you want your lives to be. Sit in this space together and use it as your new beginning.

After all your new family has been through, it is okay to take a moment. Do whatever you need to. Shut down all the outside noise and advice, this is your journey, so do what feels right for you and your family. Reach out when you need it, lean on your spouse or close family and friends. I see you and you are doing great.

# Chapter 3:

# Feeding, Burping, and

# Poop!

I am going to be frank with you, in the first few months of bringing your wee one home, you will be consumed with poop, gas, and feedings. Nothing will matter more than how much fluid goes in, and how much poop comes out. What color was it, was the poop too liquidy? Many parents have shown up at the local pharmacy in the wee hours of the morning on the hunt for more diapers and wipes without even noticing the smatterings of poo particles on their shirts. If poop isn't at the forefront of your dinner conversation, your boobs will be. Let's tackle the world of feeding first.

# Nursing

While we have a basic instinct to keep our baby alive, we know they need to be provided with nourishment, but being educated about what that looks like is key. We have discussed how each birthing journey is unique, so is each feeding journey. Each wee human is their own being with personality and temperament. Adapting to that, while informing yourself about the nutritional needs of your baby will equip you with the tools you need.

## *Colostrum*

The liquid gold of the breastfeeding world, colostrum is the first bit of "liquid" you will see coming from your nipples. It is released from your mammary glands the second you give birth. The trick here is hand expressing the colostrum, as it is thick like honey. Because of the consistency, most hospital grade breast pumps can't extract it efficiently. This thick liquid packs a punch because it is loaded in antioxidants as well as antibodies. These are key to building the precious new baby's immune system in those first days. Colostrum is low in sugar and fat, but really high in protein. It is super nutrient-dense and highly concentrated, meaning that even in small doses babies will reap all of its nutritional benefits.

Okay, that all sounds fantastic, but what is actually in it? Great question, below you will see a list of the actual ingredients found in colostrum.

- a protein that stimulates cell growth—epidermal growth factor
- lactoferrin, a protein that helps prevent infection
- leukocytes, white blood cells
- immunoglobulin A, which is an antibody
- vitamin A
- carotenoids (this is an antioxidant)
- magnesium
- copper
- zinc

More often than not, moms think they aren't producing colostrum, but on average moms have 10-20 ml of colostrum in the breast at any given time. It is the perfect set-up, because the baby only needs a small amount and this allows them a chance to learn to latch, suck, breathe, and swallow before your milk comes in.

Colostrum is the perfect cocktail for your new wee one. We know that it is working to build your baby's immune system while supplying a power packed nutritional meal. Below you will find all the benefits of colostrum.

- Easily digestible for babies.
- Coats the intestines, supplying a healthy tummy for your wee one. This prevents harmful bacteria from being absorbed.
- Keeps low blood sugar in check.
- Is a form of laxative that helps your baby clear meconium (that glorious first baby poop that resembles green tar) and reduces the chance of jaundice.
- Helps enrich and strengthen their immune system.
- Packs all the nutrition needed for your newborn.

We have established the benefits of the liquid gold, now it's time to move into breast milk. The number one question moms ask is, "When will my milk come in." Anxiously wanting to be able to provide nutrition for their baby, this is a reasonable question. Keep in mind that we are all unique, as is our milk production timeline. Your milk should arrive anywhere from day one to day four. It takes anywhere from four to eight weeks for milk supply to become established. Deciding to breastfeed your wee one, and working out the logistics is a process. You will have to dig deep into your patience stockpile and keep reminding yourself why you are doing this. For new moms, it can take four days or 35-hours to establish a solid breastfeeding routine.

Next, parents want to know if their baby is getting enough to eat. It is no surprise that we arrive home with these new bundles so anxious that we are not doing things right. Making sure they are getting enough nutrition is always high on that list. For some reason, this typically has parents believing the baby needs far more than they actually need. That first day the baby is home, they will only need 1-5 ml per feeding. Each day that number goes up by 10 ml until seven days old; then they should have 45-60 ml which is 1.5-2 oz every one-three hours for the first month. Stick to this feeding schedule and your wee one will be growing in no time.

## *Breast Milk and Bonding*

Stress builds when it comes to adequately feeding your newborn. Throw in breastfeeding and the many moving parts, we always end up with plenty of questions swirling about.

"How will I continue to breastfeed once I return to work?" "Does it hurt?" It should NOT hurt. Pain during nursing is a sign that the baby has a poor latch that is caused by a restriction or tension in the neck, jaw, and tongue. If the baby is fighting you, biting you, or there is pain, this is a sign that you need to take the baby off the nipple, and reset. Later I will give you a tip to help the baby until you can see a Lactation Consultant, Occupational Therapist, or Craniosacral Therapist that will do some mouth work.

"How do I know if they are getting enough?" Before too long, your list of questions can be a mile long. Do yourself a favor and take this one step at a time.

To begin, do your research and set short term goals. Nobody needs to put that silk "Super Mom" cape on just yet. Relax, and remember this breastfeeding journey is also a learning curve for both you and baby. Below you will find some things you can do to help be successful, less stressed, and actually enjoy your time breastfeeding.

- **Tell The World**—Once you commit to breastfeeding, tell anyone who will listen. What I actually mean is, tell those who need to support you; spouse, boss, or close friend. It is inevitable that you will struggle. Having partner support is *key* to successful breastfeeding. Their role should be clearly defined. Have them bring you the baby, prop you up with pillows, and be the "peacekeeper" when there are bumps in the road between you and your newborn. You are bringing a new human home, you will be exhausted and having support is imperative.

- **Research And Educate**—Knowledge is power here. Dive into as much research as you can. Find a local lactation consultant who will support you on this journey. Research a local breastfeeding class for both you and your partner/spouse. Empower yourself with facts.

- **Investigate Where You Are Delivering**—If you are opting for a hospital delivery, research their policies on breastfeeding support. Not all hospitals are created equal. A study conducted showed that more than 85% of moms intend on breastfeeding when they arrive at the hospital to deliver, yet only 60% are a mere three days later when they are discharged. What is happening to these hospitals for these increases to be occurring? Many hospitals have policies in place that can hinder a mom's early success for breastfeeding, including giving unnecessary formula supplementation, separating the baby from mom instead of "rooming in", and not providing moms and families with adequate support to initiate breastfeeding (Hoffman Cullinan, 2016).

- **Slow Down**—Since you found out you were going to be a parent, information has been flying past you at warp speed. When it comes to breastfeeding, slower is better. Now is the time to take a beat and find your groove. One of the mistakes most make is trying to solve a problem in a heightened state. Mom has had four hours of sleep in the last two days. She cannot remember the last time she washed her hair. The only thing on her mind currently is supplying enough nutrition to her newborn baby. Each time she attempts to breastfeed, the baby cries, pulls away, or refuses. It is 2:00 a.m. and mom is now crying as hard as the baby. This is not the time to solve this issue. It is in the quiet moments we need to begin forming the bond and figuring out the groove. Most are shocked to know that it takes eight weeks for both mom and baby to learn how to breastfeed. Each time you feel frustrated and ready to give up, remind yourself of this time frame. Remember you are not alone and the key to success is patience. Do yourself a favor and take as many quiet moments as you can find, skin-to-skin, soft voices and make that connection.

- **\*Pumping Tip\*** A trick of the trade is to establish a consistent, daily pumping time if you are committed to nursing and bottle feeding. Your body will then establish its milk supply and you will quickly achieve a few quiet moments alone.

## *Let's Talk Tongue Ties*

A tongue that has the ability to be at rest, nesting at the roof of the mouth is optimal for all ages! The tongue is the support system for the entire fascial line running from your head to your toes.

Tethered tongues are often associated with a plethora of "conditions and symptoms" ranging from physical: jaw position, crooked teeth, core stability, eye position, tip toe walking, bed wetting, sleep apnea, ear, respiratory conditions, swallowing, digestion, and development of the immune system. Tethered tongues also contribute to physiological issues like anxiety and mood disorders, intelligence, speaking, and having a sense of self.

Tongues play an important role in feeding for babies. It is vital in helping them suck and latch on to the breast properly. So what is all this talk of tongue ties, or ankyloglossia? Infant tongue tie is a congenital irregularity of the lingual frenulum that restricts movement of the tongue. It makes it difficult for newborns to create a seal and latch onto the breast. It has long been treated by frenotomy, a surgical intervention to cut the lingual frenulum (Larrain & Stevenson, 2022).

The surgery for tongue ties have been going in and out of style for decades. One can compare them to tonsillectomies. Tongue ties have been deemed one of the latest "mom trends". You cannot visit a "new parent" social media board without seeing conversations about them. All of the morning school drop-offs and yoga classes are buzzing. Baby won't sleep longer than two hours? *Have you checked for a tongue tie?* Baby has only gained half a pound? *Likely a tongue tie!* Look at this rash they have. *Check under the tongue!*

Cases of ankyloglossia have risen sharply since 2000, with the frequency of frenotomy procedures more than doubling in the US and Canada (Joseph, 2016). In Australia, the frenotomy rate jumped from 1.22 to 6.35 per 1000 live births between 1997 and 2012 (Kapoor, 2018). Most frenectomies in England are performed by lactation professionals in a private practice, so it makes it too difficult to track down solid statistics for that country.

The numbers are in folks, there is no denying the cases are on the rise, but why? Theories include such things as more families are choosing to nurse over bottle feeding, so they are more aware of the latching issue. Another theory suggests that parental awareness and education have escalated. If they notice something is off, they can type symptoms into their internet search bar. If their screens light up with tongue tying articles claiming this marvelous surgery will have your baby peaceful in no time, then guess who will make a doctor's appointment? Some other theories point toward more educated speech therapists, parents not liking the aesthetics of a tongue tie or lip tie, and wanting better overall oral health.

At the end of the day, you need to educate yourself for the sake of your wee one. This is not a mandatory surgery. One study estimated that 40 to 75 percent of babies with tongue tie will eventually breastfeed successfully without intervention. This same study also found that while frenectomies were likely to improve maternal nipple pain, they were not found to help infants with breastfeeding (Cautero, 2019).

To snip or not to snip, that is the question. Ask the questions, do all of your research, and be sure to consult with pediatric focused specialists. This will get you the full scope of what they see clinically and allow you to make the decision that is right for you and your baby.

## *Let's Talk Lip Ties*

Despite the fact that lip ties can cause issues with your baby, most physicians don't recognize them. Let's have a look at how you, as a parent can identify them and help your wee one get the help they need.

Regardless of the fact that a "lip tie" sounds ominous, it really is just that piece of skin you see when you roll up your upper lip that connects your upper lip to your upper gum. It becomes an issue, and is referred to as a lip tie, when that piece of skin is either too thick, too tight, or both.

Tongue ties are known to cause more issues with breastfeeding because it limits the tongues ability to move up. Lip ties, on the other hand, cause issues because the upper lip struggles to flare up.

Tongue ties and lip ties do not go hand-in-hand. Parents worry that if their baby has a lip tie, they will also have a tongue tie. This is not the case. Both of those areas in the mouth develop at varying times while in the womb. Can your baby have both? Yes, they can. That being said, we need to be clear that the two are not related.

It is helpful to know what signs to look for when evaluating if your baby may have a lip tie.

- wee one will have difficulties latching
- baby may cluster feed
- baby may choke on milk
- you may hear baby making a clicking sound
- they may develop jaundice
- you may notice poor weight gain
- they can be very fussy or develop colic
- your baby may seem exhausted from feeding

It is wise for breastfeeding moms to keep a close eye for clogged milk ducts, sore nipples that may look wedge shape, and a difference in your milk supply.

You may be asking yourself what you should even be looking for in your wee one's mouth. There is no need to put that added stress on you or the baby. It is always wise to have them evaluated by any member of your healthcare team. A Craniosacral Therapist, a Lactation Consultant, or a pediatric dentist can examine the mouth of your infant, and give you tips and tricks to fixing it and helping with those feeds. You most certainly can have your wee one's pediatrician look at their mouth, but be cautious because some physicians are not trained properly at diagnosing a lip tie (or its importance) in babies.

So, what happens if the lip tie is just left alone? There have been more than a few lip ties missed over the years by physicians. Today, with informed, and trained healthcare therapists, this should be a thing of the past. We are now seeing the long term effects of an undiagnosed lip tie.

- **Tooth Decay**—This is a big issue for your wee one now, and as they grow. Milk or small bits of food debris become logged in the teeth because of that upper lip. You are going to have to manually clean behind the lip to avoid this.
- **Receding gum line**—Again, if there is food or milk left sitting, trapped behind the lip, it is a breeding ground for bacteria. Over time, if this is not properly cleaned, or the lip tie is not fixed, the gum will begin to recede.
- **Braces**—You may think it is too early to be thinking of braces, but if the lip tie is not taken care of and is serious enough, your wee one may be facing years of wearing braces. If the lip tie is a grade four, meaning it is severe enough that it extends past the gums and attaches to the palate of the roof of their mouth. Over the years, and as those pearly whites begin to show, a significant gap between the teeth, especially those front ones, will appear.

- **Picky Eater**—Parents always worry when their little ones begin rejecting certain foods. Immediately dubbed "picky eaters" it can, in fact, be due to a lip tie at times. If one was never detected, it can make eating some foods difficult. If it is severe enough it can even affect their ability to clear off a fork or spoon, or properly chew. All of this can present itself as a child who is just another picky eater.

## How Is a Lip Tie Corrected?

For this procedure, you should be heading to a pediatric dentist, not the doctor. The procedure is called a frenectomy. The entire ordeal should only take a few minutes, but be sure to have a sit down visit to discuss and ask any questions. The goal is for you and the baby to feel comfortable. It is required that your wee one stay very still throughout this procedure, but many do not like to restrain the baby, as it can be traumatizing for both parents and wee one. There are options available here, be sure to ask about them. If you are comfortable with it, you can even lay in the dentist chair, and the baby can lay on you.

The first step will include having a numbing solution rubbed onto the area. This makes things more comfortable for the baby. Next, a small, handheld laser is used to quickly, and efficiently, snip the piece of skin, properly connecting the lip to the gums.

As mentioned, the procedure takes minutes, and once done, the baby is free to be showered with cuddles and love. Some want to be breastfed immediately, and that is okay. Don't expect an immediate improvement in latch, as their muscle memory will have to be retrained with the new mouth setup.

It is extremely important to have follow-up visits with your Craniosacral Therapist and have them teach you stretches for baby's mouth. You are going to want to do these multiple times a day. By pulling up on the baby's lip and applying gentle massage to the area, you will prevent it from growing back. Your therapist will give you step-by-step instructions on this.

## *Feeding and Reflux*

Oh the wonderful world of baby spit up. Reflux is pretty common in babies. Although it is common, that doesn't mean that it is okay or normal. Reflux is a symptom of dysfunction, tension, nervous system imbalance, birth trauma, and a poor latch. There is HELP for reflux, and most doctors will not offer that information. Most are just quick to offer the nasty medication, which isn't that effective.

Just over half of all newborns will experience some level of reflux. A bit of throw up on your shoulder after eating. A couple extra burps, or just all around cranky. But what exactly is reflux anyway?

Have you ever bent over to tie your shoes and that liquid that resembles hot lava comes spilling up into your throat? No? Well, consider yourself lucky. Reflux occurs when food actually backs up into the esophagus (or throat as I just referred to it), from the stomach. We have all held that child who spits up just looking at them. It can happen multiple times a day, but as long as they are growing and content, there is no issue.

Unfortunately, there are those who will suffer, arch their backs in pain, and spit up almost every time they eat. They will have trouble maintaining a healthy weight. So, we now know what reflux is, but what causes it?

Reflux is usually from restriction in the baby's nervous system that involves several nerves for swallowing. Another known source is neck tension from either torticollis or tongue restriction. We know that it is also caused by the lower esophageal sphincter not closing tightly, allowing stomach contents and yummy digestive juices to travel up.

Oftentimes new parents are told not to be overly concerned, that baby will outgrow this by 18 months of age. But, there are things you can do to help alleviate the symptoms.

- Don't overfeed your wee human. Watch for hunger cues and only feed on demand.
- Be the M.V.P. of your burp game. It is recommended to burp after each ounce instead of waiting until the end.
- No more feeding lying down. You should always be feeding the baby at a 45 degree angle. I understand this one won't be easy, but do your best to keep the baby upright for 30-minutes after eating.

Dealing with eating issues can be stressful for both parents and baby. Don't hesitate to reach out to your healthcare team if you feel your wee one needs an examination. If you ever see bright yellow, green, or blood in their spit up, seek immediate medical attention.

# The Wonderful World of Poop

If there is one thing we can all agree on, with babies comes poop—so much poop! If you were squeamish before becoming a parent, you will get over it quickly. Before too long, you will have a "nose" for the surprises your wee one has left for you, or if their tummy is upset. Don't be shocked when you are having in-depth discussions with your friends about color, consistency, and regularity of your baby's bowel movements.

In all honesty, your newborn's poop is like a window into their overall health. On those multiple trips to your healthcare provider, they too will be asking plenty of questions about your baby's stool. Just remember, all those dirty diapers you are changing is a great indicator that they are not dehydrated or constipated.

While discussing poop, we shouldn't miss talking about the "first" poop. Many uninformed parents have been shocked when opening that diaper, having no idea why they were staring at a thick, black, mess resembling tar. This is called meconium, it is normal and should pass after about three days. I thought it might be insightful to have a literal "poop chart" to help you know approximate bowel movements at different stages.

| Type of Feeding | Days 1-3 | First 6 Weeks | After Starting Solids |
|---|---|---|---|
| Breastfed | Meconium will pass 36-48 hours after birth. It will change to yellow/green color by day four. | About three bowel movements per day, runny and yellow in color. Could be more for some babies. This will taper off to every other day. | More frequent, solid bowel movements once solids are introduced. |
| Formula fed | same as above | Greenish/light brown stool. 1-4 poops per day. After one month, it should taper off to every other day. | 1-2 poops per day |

Keep in mind that your baby's stool is a chart into their health. If you suddenly notice a sour smell, mucous, or anything else out of the ordinary, don't hesitate to reach out to your healthcare professional. It could be something as simple as a new food, but it could be an allergy or virus. Always err on the side of caution.

Be sure you visit the section near the end of this book titled "Magic Tips and Tricks" where you will find valuable and insightful advice on feeding, reflux, and poop! Brought to you by the professional baby whisperer, and author of this book. With 20 years of experience, you will want to read her proven and helpful advice.

# Chapter 4:

# Head Shape & Tummy Time

Now that we have waded through the poop and breastmilk situation, let's talk about all things tummy time! Long gone are the days when the precious wee one would be placed on their backs and no more thought was given to it. I know when I was a child (think before the internet...way before), there was no talk of baby development before they started crawling or walking. That has changed a great deal.

# The Importance of Tummy Time

The American Academy of Pediatrics established guidelines in 1994, informing us that it is safest for babies to sleep on their backs. What that means though, is that infants spend up to 15 hours a day staring at the ceiling. As a result, babies have fewer opportunities to practice using their arms, back, neck, and head to lift themselves up (Berk, 2020).

How important tummy time is to your new bundle cannot be overemphasized here. So why is that? Most parents believe that it is merely to help strengthen their neck muscles. In fact, tummy time helps us develop the following.

- gross motor skills
  - Baby holding their chest up in the prone position.
  - Wee one rolling from their stomach to their back.
  - Watch how they develop tone in their neck for strength.
- fine motor skills
  - It helps encourage random movements of their arms and legs.
  - Helps initiate play with rattles, mirrors, and pictures.
- eye control
  - Place a picture on the floor where the baby can see it. Move the picture to the

right, then to the left. You will see the
baby's eyes move to the right first,
followed by the head and shoulders.
Patiently, and slowly, move the picture
again. Watch as the baby looks away, then
looks back at the image. When they are re-
engaged, move it again. Great exercise!

- body stabilization
  - This stimulates the nervous system. Motor
    development moves from head to toe, and
    then trunk to extremities.

## *Important Things to Remember*

Tummy time can be a great time to bond with your new
wee one, but keep in mind, there are important things to
remember. Start early and do it often. Many times,
parents are afraid to begin too early, thinking they may
harm the neck muscles. You are safe, and so is your baby.
Those times when you are making a connection, skin-to-
skin, are a great opportunity to allow them to start
practicing. When they begin pulling their faces up and
away from you, they are engaging in the beginning stages
of tummy time.

That being said, tummy time should always be well
supervised until the baby has good head control and can
roll over by themselves. We want this to be a pleasant and
fun experience for both baby and parents, so start slow
and build. Just start with one minute and increase by 15-
second intervals each time. Most babies will immediately
cry the second you place them face down. If this happens,

don't panic and scoop the baby up immediately. Generally, it means they have already figured out that if they make sounds, they receive lots of ooey gooey love and attention. Wait out the minute, it will be worth it.

We should be making a solid effort to engage in tummy time five to six times per day. Did you just read that and say out loud, "Are you kidding me, I do not have time for that, I barely have time to shower!" I hear you, and I understand. Try to remember that these sessions should only be for a minute in the beginning. Also, don't be shy about tag teaming in the other parent, grandparent, dog walker, or Amazon delivery man. Well, okay maybe not the last two, unless you really enjoy their company!

You can get creative here with tummy time. Some other options can include the following.

- Use a large exercise ball and have the baby supported on their tummy.
- Grab that nursing pillow and lay your bundle of joy across it.
- Try reverse tummy time! Place your baby's back supported fully on your lap with their head just tipping away from your knees towards the floor into a fully supported baby cervical stretch. Remember to hold them securely. Just 15 seconds is a lot!

Now, lay out the blanket and let's rock this tummy time.

One thing to keep in mind when engaging in tummy time with your wee one, less is more. Oftentimes, we will roll the baby over onto their tummy, and the second they begin to fuss, we pull out every toy imaginable to attempt to entertain them.

What researchers are finding is that by showering them with so many options, we are overwhelming them. The study, from the University of Toledo, Ohio observed 36 toddlers, ages 18-30 months in free play sessions. The wee ones were either in the group with four toys, or the group with sixteen toys. The study showed a significant difference in the two groups. The wee ones in the group with only four toys showed a greater quality of play. Essentially this study showed that when given fewer toys, the babies played with them in more varied ways, for a longer length of time and it improved their cognitive development (Newman, 2017).

# Baby's Head Shape

As if you didn't have enough on your plate with poop color, feedings, and tummy time. Now you have to be mindful of flat spots on your wee one's head. Wait…what did you just say? My perfect and beautiful baby could have a misshapen head? What causes this and how do we deal with it?

## *What Causes Flat Spots on Baby's Head*

The most common cause is the way the baby sleeps. We have all been advised that for the safety of the wee one, they need to sleep on their back. Now add up all the hours they sleep, flat on their back, and flat on their melon. We can't forget, before they have enough strength in their neck, they are also in car seats, swings, bouncy seats, and all those fancy gadgets we discussed earlier. Their tiny wee heads lay flat against those as well.

Premature babies are at a higher risk of developing a flat head. They still have very soft skulls, and spend significant amounts of time laying on their backs not being picked up because of their individual medical needs.

Below you will see some terms to describe different types of flat spots.

- Plagiocephaly
  - The head has a flat spot on the back of ONE side, causing the head to push forward, bring the ear forward, and the opposing eye to narrow.
  - Babies with plagiocephaly will prefer turning their heads to the right 70-80% of the time for both full term and premature babies. This can greatly contribute to torticollis, difficulty swallowing, as well as create difficulty for babies to track with their eyes for balanced head control.
  - With early interventions by a therapeutic team–Physiotherapist, Occupational therapist, Craniosacral therapist, Chiropractor–and feeding specialists treatments, you can quickly facilitate corrections!

- Facial asymmetries can correct for up to 18 months, however this may always persist even with treatments.
- Deformity closer to the base of the skull/neck corrects more slowly over several months.
- Causes include tongue tie, torticollis, sleep positioning, multiple births, and early head down position.
- Plagiocephaly has been proven at 36 months to have lower development scores in areas of adaptive behaviors, language, and cognition.

- Scaphocephaly
  - The back of the head has flattened on both sides but widens at the back, increasing the front to back length of the head which changes the center of gravity; affects balance and righting the head position on the neck. This position creates what we term "cervical extension".
  - When we see this in preterm babies, they are 10 times weaker than a full term baby.
  - There are also a bunch of cranium specific imbalances that happen including compression of the vagus nerve, changes in vision, auditory (hearing), and vestibular system (balance) functions,

affecting the venous system with the cranium.

- Brachycephaly
  - The entire backside of their head has flattened. This is caused by the positional sleep position on their back.
- Overlapping Cranial Bones
  - Cranial bones are designed to help babies get out of the birth canal. Bones can overlap 4/10-8/10 inches at birth. Although not super common, overlapping bones can be painful for babies.

## *How to Prevent Flat Spots*

We have already discussed the importance of tummy time. This is a great opportunity to give your wee one a well-deserved break from being on their back and to begin strengthening their neck muscles. But what else can we do to prevent these flat spots?

I did a quick search on Amazon and found a few pillows designed to retrofit into your car seat, stroller, or bouncy seat. They claim to help your wee one avoid flat spots, and are ergonomically designed, but guess what? There are no studies found anywhere proving these help; trust me I triple checked. What is even more important, I mean extremely important, is that there is no clinical recommendation for them because they actually restrict the baby's range of motion. We strongly discourage the use of them.

What other great tools are available to help you, help your baby?

- Switch it up! Try changing up the positions in the crib. Take a look at how you place your wee one in the crib. If you are a right-handed parent, you likely carry your baby in their left arm and place them down with the head to their left. When they are in this position, they must turn to the right to peer out into the room. Try to be mindful of placing your wee one in their crib to encourage active turning of the head to the side that's not flattened. Babies are nosey creatures, so this should encourage them to turn their head to see what actions they may be missing.

- Have more baby cuddles. If you are exhausted and need some time for you, bring in the backups. We need to limit the time a baby spends lying on their back, whether that is in the crib, car seat, swing, or fancy bouncy seat. We all know that feeling, baby has been awake most of the night. You take them for a nice walk, and, like magic, they are fast asleep. You begin dreaming of a hot shower and a thirty minute nap. Unfortunately, leaving the baby sleeping in the stroller is only going to make that flat spot worse. Instead, why not place the baby on you, chest-to-chest and you can both have a nap. Keeping the baby off their head as much as possible throughout the day will keep pressure off the flat spot.

- Change the baby's head position while they sleep. I know, never wake a sleeping baby. That isn't the intention here. We just want to gently move the head, slowly from left to right, then back again.

- Babies are curious by nature, that is why they are always looking around. To promote continuous head and neck movement, try strategically placing or hanging some unique things for them to look at. This can be as simple as hanging a feather duster, or a brightly colored balloon at an angle you wish for them to turn.

- You will find times when it is difficult to keep your baby centered and not slouching when in their car seat, stroller, or baby seat. If you are finding that your wee one needs extra support to keep them from slouching in their car seat, here is a trick. You can safely strap them in, just as you regularly do. Check to make sure their straps are snug. At this point, you want to be sure your baby is straightened as much as possible. Now, grab a receiving blanket or small towel and roll it tightly. You are going to want to place one on either side of your wee one. Place this right along their body from their ear right down to their bum. This won't interfere with the function of the car seat and is what Certified Child Passenger Safety Technicians (CPST) recommend doing for babies who need a little more support.

Keep in mind that a lot of the babies with flat spots on their head will show some degree of torticollis. Visiting a Craniosacral Therapist, Pediatric Physical Therapist, Pediatric Chiropractor, or a Pediatric Occupational Therapist and establishing a home exercise program will be beneficial. They can teach you exercises to do with your baby involving stretching. Most moves involve stretching the neck to the side opposite the tilt. In time, the neck muscles will get longer and the neck will straighten itself out. The exercises are simple, but must be done correctly.

The optimal time for reversing flat spots is between 0-2 months of age, as their cranial plates are developing and are still super squishy. It is discouraging to know that oftentimes parents are told, by doctors, that these flat spots are fine and will resolve themselves. They need immediate attention. The recommendation by Physiotherapists, Occupational Therapists, and Craniosacral Therapists is 0-2 months to avoid the use of helmets.

Always remember, this can be remedied. Do your research and choose the path that best suits you and your baby. Your healing team will have you both feeling better about your wee ones melon in no time.

## Chapter 5:

# Sleep

*Don't talk to me right now, I was up all night keeping my parents awake and I am exhausted!*—Anonymous

Welcome to the world of Zombieland. Well that is at least how it feels to most new parents. Of all the things that change when a baby enters our world, this is usually the one thing that most notice first. The lack of sleep and how much of a shock to the system that is.

# Why Is Sleep So Important?

It seems to be that once our wee ones make it out into this world, we become obsessed with getting them to sleep "through" the night. Did you actually know that even before they are born by about 30-34 weeks gestation, they are cycling through sleep patterns? Before embarking on their journey outside the womb, babies spend almost 95% of their time sleeping. That doesn't change much in those first few weeks at home. How often do you hear your friends and family say, "Every time I come to visit, the baby is sleeping."

It is a massive undertaking going from that safe and warm womb and into the world they will now live in. They need their rest because this is where the real work is going to begin. Their wee little bodies and brains are in a rapid pattern of development. While those tiny little eyelids are fluttering closed, their brain tissue is growing and developing, they are storing memories, synapses are being established, connections are forming, and wow are they ever trying to restore those energy reserves!

Life truly is a miracle, and watching a baby sleep is even more so. A wee ones brain will double in size during that first year. Pretty much all of that will happen while those tiny eyelids are closed. Babies need an average of 14-18 hours of sleep per night, according to their age. Below you will find some insights into why that sleep is so critical.

- If a baby endures consistent lack of sleep, it can lead to much bigger problems as they get older.

These can include developmental delays, or cognitive problems.

- I find it fascinating to know that while a baby is busy during the day, meeting new people, seeing and hearing new things, those memories are all stored and formed during sleep.
- Brain synapses (circuits that connect your nervous system to your brain, signals to tell your brain, ouch that hurts) are formed during sleep. Get ready for this stat, more than 1,000,000 million neural connections are formed every second, up until their third birthday. (Athena, 2020).
- As we mentioned, most of the wee human's brain will develop as they sleep. What you may not know is that the connections between the right and left hemispheres of the brain also happen during sleep.

We can all agree that sleep is vital to a newborn. A well-rested baby will be more receptive to feeding, be more responsive, and be much easier to soothe. We can conclude that a wee human who gets lots of sleep will be happier, and so will you!

## Sleep Cycles

Figuring out the magical formula to get your new baby to sleep will, at times, consume you. If you find yourself startled awake, realizing that precious baby slept five hours straight, you will trace your steps in an attempt to repeat the evening and an encore performance.

The fact of the matter is, it can take a while to understand your baby's sleep cycles. It can help to keep a small journal handy to keep notes on any patterns you begin to notice. After the beginning weeks of constant feedings and chaos slows down, you may begin to see a pattern of eat-sleep-play. Try to write down the times of day you notice these patterns.

It is also a great idea to begin a pre-sleep routine. This routine is just as important for naps, as it is for bedtime. It can consist of a nice, soothing bath, followed by a warm swaddle, feed, cuddle/rock, and down for sleep. Your routine will be suited for your needs, the key here is consistency. The more you continue to do the same things, the sooner your baby will know that this is a precursor to sleep.

A pro tip for laying your baby down in the crib is always lead feet first, placing baby's bum down and then lay the head head down. Once your baby is in the crib, lay your hand on their stomach or rhythmically pat; either of these things will help settle baby quicker.

So, what exactly are the different sleep cycles of a baby? Below you can find three different sleep cycles and what to expect from your baby during them.

### *Quiet Sleep or Deep Sleep*

- lack of body, facial and eye movement
- smooth breathing
- eyes are closed tightly
- sucking bursts
- occasionally startles

- difficult to wake baby
- if baby wakes up, they are quick to fall back to sleep
- feeding is unsuccessful

## *Active Sleep or Light Sleep*

- irregular breathing
- baby can smile
- REM sleep
- easy to wake baby
- feeding can be difficult
- baby is more responsive

## *Drowsy*

- eyes may be open or closed or glazed
- easier to wake baby
- difficult to tell if baby is asleep or awake
- if left alone, they might fall back to sleep
- feeding may be difficult until fully awake
- can awaken or go back to sleep

By learning as much as you can about your baby's sleep cycles, you can limit the amount of frustration of both you and the baby.

# Physical Reasons Your Baby Can't Sleep

We all know there are countless reasons for wee ones to wake throughout the night. But what are some of the common physical reasons for keeping them up at night? Let's talk about oral reasons that could be complicating your baby's sleep. Oral restrictions interfere with oral and tongue function. You wouldn't think so, but good sleep does rely on tongue positioning. We need to determine if your baby has a tongue, lip, or buccal tie. I have compiled a list below to help you know exactly what to look for.

- baby has an open mouth with low tongue position
- taking a long time to fall asleep
- parents helping baby to sleep
- baby wakes too frequently
- waking consistently between 30-40 minutes
- snoring or other breathing noises
- flailing arms or moving around a lot

If you suspect that your wee human may have an oral restriction, don't hesitate to seek advice from your healthcare team.

# What Is Sleeping Through the Night?

You might be surprised to hear this, but your precious new baby is actually designed to wake up multiple times throughout the night. Aside from the many feedings they will need, they are actually also wanting and needing their parents. Yes, you heard that correctly. Those sweet little faces will wake up in order to be with either, or both of their parents throughout the night. It has been proven that being with you helps to regulate their blood pressure, heart rate, and body temperature.

What most don't realize is that babies are not born with a shiver response. Until the age of six months, they do not shiver when they are cold. Newborns are born with a certain type of fat to help keep them warm, but they will still wake and cry out for you to maintain body temperature.

The actual term "sleeping through the night" is defined as 12:00 a.m.–5:00 a.m. for infants. Most babies nurse to sleep and wake at least 1-3 times during the night for the first year or so.

Establishing good bedtime routines is imperative. Keeping the nursery at a comfortable temperature for sleeping, and the lighting low is key. When the baby wakes in the night, do your best not to engage too much as to wake your wee one fully. If they become fussy, try practicing the power of the "shush" to calm them.

Newborns and young babies are not fond of silence. They just spent months in the womb, where there is constant whooshing, some say louder than a vacuum. They are happier, and calm easier when there is noise. Keep in mind though, that not all noise is the same to babies.

If the baby is upset, fussy, or crying, hold them in your arms and on their side. Gently swaying, place your lips against their ear and shush. The general rule of thumb is to shush as loudly as they are crying. As they calm, and their cry quiets, so should your shush.

Don't underestimate the incredible power of the shush!

You can purchase sound machines that mimic this sound, and they work wonders if you play them while the baby is sleeping. Try to avoid the ones that mimic the sound of fans or waves, as they may not be the pitch baby needs.

Fret not, even though it feels like you will never sleep again, before you know it, your wee one will be a teenager sleeping 18 hours a day!

## Chapter 6:

# Postpartum Family

Here we are, all back home living our best life and adapting to being parents. Guess what, this is not like the movies. Why is it that nobody on T.V. seems to be waddling to the bathroom because of a painful episiotomy? There are never any sinks filled with dishes from four days ago, or laundry covering the bedroom floor. I don't know about you, but this household is exhausted. But what if it's more than just exhaustion? Postpartum affects us all differently and both you and your partner need to be checking in with each other throughout it all.

There are important conversations you both should be having during this time as well. Creating life, then giving birth, (if that is the way you brought your bundle into this world) takes a huge toll on you, physically and mentally. A contraceptive plan should be discussed well in advance of resuming sexual activity. Closely spaced or unintended births are a health concern because they are associated with an increase in maternal, newborn, and child morbidity and mortality. The recommended duration between the next pregnancy is a minimum 24 months. This is based on a consultation by the World Health Organization (WHO), in order to reduce the risk of adverse maternal, perinatal, and infant deaths. Even with these statistics, 61% of women are not using safe and effective contraception within 24 months of giving birth to avoid an unintended pregnancy (Moore et al., 2015).

# A Deeper Look Into Postpartum Recovery

Growing a human is hard work. Adopting a baby is hard work. Having a surrogate carry your baby is hard work. No matter how you manifested your wee one here, you are now a parent. Forty weeks of worry, exhaustion, diaper-buying, and excitement. Most assume the hard work ends here. I would like you to take a moment and think about how much you all have been through up to this point. The planning and preparing, the hormone rushes, and lack of sleep. The changes to the body and to your home. It is completely normal to expect a bit of a downhill slide for some.

## *What Does Postpartum Look Like for Women?*

Let's start this off by making it very clear, no two women are the same. Do not let your best friend find you knuckle deep in the ice cream because you have been stalking your next door neighbor on social media all day. Yes, she did have a baby the same week as you, and yes her profile does have her doing Mommy & Me yoga classes three times a week. We also have no clue what her life is like the other four days and maybe those yoga classes are all that is keeping her together.

Now, let's stay focused on you. Regardless of the delivery you had, the first six weeks after delivery is considered your postpartum period. Your body needs you to rest, relax, and heal as much as humanly possible. You grew an actual human, take a breath, okay.

Let's talk vaginas. Oh those wondrous vessels! You are probably asking yourself, or any close friends…how long is this going to cause me this much pain? A few things factor in here. If you had a vaginal birth and were lucky enough not to tear your perineum, you are looking at about three weeks. If you did tear, or had an episiotomy, hold on tight for six weeks. I know, I am clenching my gluteus maximus as I recall it myself. Keep in mind, if you are the recipient of an episiotomy, numbness in that area is a common symptom reported for months past delivery.

Pro-tip, before you head in for delivery, buy yourself some cheap maxi pads from the dollar store, soak them in water and roll them up as tight as you can. Place each one individually in a sandwich or freezer bag and toss them in the freezer. These vagina popsicles will be your best friend when you get home. Pop one out, and gently lay it wherever you need some instant relief. I kid you not, some moms have been known to keep a small cooler beside their bed during those first few days.

So many moms want to ask "the questions" but are too shy. That, or maybe they are afraid to hear the answer. Will my vagina ever be the same again? It may vary slightly, but honestly, not enough for you to notice. You and your vagina are going to be just fine.

If you deliver via C-section, you can expect approximately 4-6 weeks of recovery time. The key is to keep moving each day, a little further than the day before. No heavy lifting until your doctor allows.

Let's talk about bleeding. Oftentimes, new moms are not given enough information regarding postpartum bleeding. They wind up terrified that something is wrong. So, how much blood is too much? Most are shocked to find out that bleeding for up to six weeks is normal. It will be like a heavier period, containing leftover blood, mucus, and tissue from your uterus. Day three to ten is when you will find it the heaviest, then you should notice it letting up. The color should begin to change as well, from a bright red, to a pink, then brown, and finally a yellowish-white. One of the biggest concerns is always, "How will I know if I am bleeding too much?" The general rule here is, if you are soaking through a pad more than once an hour, or if you notice large clots, seek medical attention.

## How Can I Heal Faster?

Those first few days will likely be the worst. To help ease the perineal area, ice, ice, and more ice. Grab those vagina popsicles as often as possible. You want to keep the area clean as well, so spraying warm water over the area after urinating will help prevent any infections. Try to avoid excessively long standing or sitting, and try to sleep on your side.

If you have a C-section incision, be sure to get instructions for care and cleaning. What to use on the incision, (typically just water) and at what point you should leave it uncovered. Avoid lifting anything heavy.

For overall aches and pains, indulge yourself in a nice, hot bath, a massage, or try using a heating pad.

We can't forget about the poop. That first bowel movement after giving birth is an adventure. Tears are shed, cries for help can be heard for miles. Okay, it's not that bad. In all honesty, don't force it. Eat lots of fruits and vegetables high in fiber, take the baby out for walks, and use a gentle stool softener. Absolutely no straining when nature calls.

Even though it may be a while before you can do any actual exercise, your vagina is ready, willing, and able. Kegels are the best way to get your vagina back into pre-baby shape. They will help with postpartum urinary incontinence, so that's a bonus. You should be aiming for three sets of ten in the first two weeks, then increase it to three sets of twenty from there.

The BEST piece of advice to get back to pre-baby form is to seek out a physical therapist who specializes in pelvic floor health. You will thank me!

It is important to keep all your doctor's appointments. They will be checking on your incisions, removing your stitches if you had a C-section, and checking in on how you are feeling emotionally.

I have included a small list of things you will want on hand before you deliver. You will thank yourself for being prepared.

- Maxi pads for the famous vagina popsicles, and of course for the postpartum bleeding. No tampons allowed at this stage.

- Sitz bath, the wonderful little tub designed for you to sit in and soak your perineal area. It aids in the healing.
- Ice or gel packs. The amount of ways to ice your perineal area is amazing. The good old bag of frozen peas, to our homemade frozen maxipad padsicles.
- Cotton panties, a.k.a. granny panties because comfort is key. Not to mention, who wants to ruin expensive, pretty, panties with all that postpartum bleeding?
- Acetaminophen for body aches and pains, as well as perineal pain. Check with your doctor.
- If you are breastfeeding, grab some nursing pads. They will keep your leaking nipples from ruining your favorite pajamas.
- Perineum or squirt bottle. If you don't have one, get one. The thought of "wiping" will have you wincing. These will bring comfort and cleanliness. Simply pour warm water over the perineal area after urinating to avoid infection.
- Witch hazel pads are amazing when used with ice packs to help with hemorrhoids and vaginal pain.
- Heating pad to help with the pain in your breasts or all over body pain.
- Stool softeners just may become your best friend. In those first few days, pushing at all is painful, so do yourself a favor and don't.

- Cracked nipple cream, yep it is a thing. There is plenty on the market so shop around for your favorite.
- Nursing bras, I really want to suggest investing in some comfortable, great fitting ones. You will thank yourself.

Now you should be more than prepared for rapid postpartum healing and gentle recovery.

## *What You Need to Know About Postpartum Depression*

After you finally give birth to your baby, you can find yourself dealing with a slew of intense emotions. One moment you can be feeling excitement and joy, and the next, anger and anxiety. However, it can also result in something unexpected—depression.

Majority of new moms will experience something termed postpartum "baby blues" after giving birth. This usually includes anxiety, crying spells, moodiness, and trouble sleeping. Baby blues usually begin within the first two or three days after delivery, and can last up to two weeks.

I know we touched on this earlier, but the seriousness of it warrants a more in depth discussion. There are some new moms who experience a much more severe form of depression known as Postpartum depression. This lasts a lot longer than baby blues.

PPD does not mean you are weak, or that you are not maternal. Unfortunately most moms suffer in silence because they cannot understand why they are not happy.

This is supposed to be the happiest time of their life. Why are they so unbelievably sad? The key to beating this is prompt treatment.

So, what are the signs to watch out for? If you are concerned about your partner, friend or loved one, you will find signs of baby blues and PPD below. If you are a new mom, and you are concerned for yourself, read the list, and do not be ashamed to ask for help. It takes a village.

## Signs of Baby Blues

Below you will find a list of observations to keep watch for. Typically, these symptoms should only last from a few days to a couple of weeks.

- crying
- irritability
- reduced concentration
- anxiety
- trouble sleeping
- mood swings
- sadness
- appetite problems
- feeling overwhelmed

## Signs of Postpartum Depression

Below you will find a list of observations to keep watch for when you are concerned things have progressed to PPD. The symptoms last longer and are more severe than the baby blues. It can become so severe, you are unable to care for your baby or yourself. If left untreated, it can last for many months, or even a year after giving birth.

- excessive crying
- loss of appetite or eating too much
- loss of energy or overwhelming fatigue
- sleeping all the time or can't sleep at all
- severe mood swings
- withdrawing from everyone
- can't bond with baby
- panic attacks and severe anxiety
- thoughts of death or suicide
- hopelessness
- don't believe you are a good mother, don't deserve your baby
- thoughts of harming yourself or your baby
- restlessness
- can't think clear or make decisions
- no interest in activities you use to enjoy
- feel shame, guilt, and inadequate
- intense anger

These are all large and intimidating feelings. The thoughts of bringing your new baby home and then not wanting to engage in this new life is devastating. We need to advocate for better education in this area so new parents feel safe and comfortable getting the help they need. This is treatable, please reach out.

## *Postpartum Depression in Men*

We cannot possibly forget about dads in this scenario. It is absurd to me that it has taken this long for people to sit up and realize that men are going through a plethora of emotions as well. Yes, new fathers can experience PPD, too. They are coining the term PPND, which stands for Parental Postpartum Depression.

Why is it that it has taken so long for this to be uncovered, you may ask? Simple, men find it extremely difficult to discuss their emotions and feelings. We are slowly trying to break down those barriers of "man up" and "men don't cry" stigmas allowing them to express and deal with their emotions. This is a move in the right direction, because the statistics are in, and they are startling.

A report in the Journal of American Medical Association has discovered that 10% of men worldwide have displayed signs of depression. This started from the first trimester of their partner's pregnancy through six months after birth. This number jumped to an astounding 26% during the three-to-six-month period after the baby's birth (Rosen, 2020).

Will Courtenay, Licensed Clinical Social Worker (LCSW) and founder of the website PostpartumMen.com says, "One in four new dads in the United States will suffer from depression—that amounts to 3000 dads each day." After studying cases more closely, he concludes that the best indicator of a man's risk for depression is if his wife is suffering with PPD. An estimated 50% of men who have a wife who is depressed, are suffering from depression as well (Rosen, 2020). This situation is one that needs immediate action. Having both parents with mental health issues and a new baby can lead to significant strain on the relationship.

Many assume the symptoms of PPD for dad's is the same as it is for moms. Although there are some similarities, you will find a list below of symptoms specific to dads.

- heart palpitations
- shortness of breath
- abusing alcohol, drugs, gambling, or extra marital affairs
- not wanting to engage in sex
- not feeling worthy
- sadness, anger, irritability

As we discussed with PPD and new moms, not all dads are created equal either. You know the men in your life better than anyone else. If you notice them acting differently, withdrawing, or an overall aura of sadness, let them know you are there for them.

## *Mental Health and Self-Care*

Asking for help is not as easy as most would think. It is a confusing time when mental health comes knocking on our doors. That is especially true when we are just starting a family. Bringing a bundle of joy through the doors elicits images of baby giggles and family photo shoots in the backyard; people are often confused when we are depressed instead of leaping for joy.

Now is the time to remember how important you are and put the focus back on your health. You are both going to be parents now, for life. You will need a lot of energy and fuel for that undertaking. We have listed all the ways you can take care of your physical being, below you will find all the ways you need to take care of your mental well-being.

Cami Hill, from Intermountain Healthcare uses the acronym **SNOWBALL** to remind you of some helpful tips for better mental health.

## S is for Sleep

We do not give enough credit to our sleeping habits. Our body recovers and refuels during sleep. It is valuable and needed. If your body or brain is tired, rest, nap, do whatever you need to get that much needed sleep.

## N is for Nutrition

Making time to eat well can be a challenge with a newborn at home. Dumping empty calories into your body just adds to the cycle of fatigue and exhaustion. Fueling up with nutritional food will help you heal faster and is even more important if mama bear is breastfeeding.

## O is for Omega 3 Fatty Acids

If anxiety or depression is getting in your way of daily tasks, you want to eat foods high in this. Mackerel and salmon are the highest, but if you are not a big fan of seafood, grab some flax or chia seeds. Even walnuts are a great source.

## W is For Walking

Depression can leave you wanting to stay under the covers, hiding from the world. We now know that getting your body moving and releasing those feel good endorphins helps improve mood. A change of scenery is wonderful for mental cleansing too.

### B is For Breaks From Baby

Many parents have trouble being away from the new bundle. Taking breaks away will do both baby and parent wonders. A nice drive with the music playing, a spa day, or even grocery shopping without a baby. Just time for you.

### A is For Adult Time

You can easily lose sight of who you were before becoming a parent. The relationships and friendships that helped define you. Keeping in touch will help guide you through this rough patch. Continue to make plans, lunch dates, and don't forget those important date nights. Try not to add stress by making these too elaborate. If all you can handle is ordering in a pizza and watching a movie, that is okay.

### L is For Laughter

When was the last time you laughed? There will be times you have to remind yourself that we need laughter. Pop some delicious popcorn and watch a comedy. Call that friend of yours who always has you laughing until it hurts. Remember to laugh.

## L is For Liquids

Water, the elixir of the gods…or something like that. I know it seems that people are always saying to drink more water. There must be some merit to it. You need to be drinking a lot of water. Grab yourself a water bottle that makes you happy. How about one with sweary words, or a monkey eating watermelon—that would make me laugh. Keep it filled all day and refuel that mind, body, and soul.

# How to Ask For Help

Hormones are raging, sleep is minimal at best, and you fear you have Postpartum depression. As if you weren't dealing with enough, you now have to decide how to get help. It can feel easier to keep it to yourself because once you speak about it, you have to deal with it. Uttering those words, depression, anxiety, sadness—gives it life. You don't want to feel judged or shamed, so understandably, keeping it quiet seems easier. If you do, it will get worse. It is okay to tell yourself that you are worth happiness. You are worth healing, and you are worth help.

Your first step should be sitting down with your partner, or someone you feel can support you. This can stir up feelings of anxiety or fear. You may question if they are going to understand this or judge you. The best way to begin may be to offer up some knowledge. Be prepared with what PPD is, some statistics and symptoms. They likely have a pretty good idea of what is going on, but hearing it from you will put them at ease. Tell them how you have been feeling and that you want the help to feel better. Next, should be a call to your doctor. They are well rehearsed in PPD and can begin to put a plan in place. If you have a Nutritionist, Chiropractor, Craniosacral, or Physical Therapist, it would be beneficial to bring them all into your healing team. Together they can create a nurturing, healing, path specific to you.

Be gentle with yourself. This is a huge first step, acknowledge that.

## *Calling All Helpers*

When they said it takes a village, they really were on to something. Raising a child takes time, energy, and a lot of adjustment. It is best to spend those first few days together as a family. Finding a rhythm of what works, or doesn't, is essential. Allowing yourselves this time may uncover places you need help. If you find you cannot refuel or re-energize with the sleep you need, there likely is a grandparent, auntie, or best friend eagerly waiting to step in. Let them! Trying to do it all will cause burn-out, or worse, and you won't be doing yourself or your baby any good. Talk to your partner too. Are they feeling worn down trying to tackle all the household chores? Would they rather be bonding with their new bundle as well? Remember all of those offers of help in these times. Family and friends really want to pitch in. Let them roll up their sleeves and take care of the dishes or cleaning. Let Mom come over and make dinner. Taking those daily tasks off your plate for a while will feel like a weight has been lifted.

If you feel those moments of guilt creeping in, those thoughts of "I should be able to handle all of this," press the pause button. Take a moment and ask yourself, if someone I loved had a baby and needed me, what would I do? Would you judge them or think they were not a wonderful mom? Of course not, you would be delighted that they asked. So, get out of your own way and allow those who love you the opportunity to help.

# The Relationship With Your Partner

It is inevitable, your relationship is going to change once you bring a baby home. Parenthood brings with it a lack of sleep, hormone changes, stress, anxiety, just to name a few. Your focus moves from that loving relationship to keeping a human alive and sneaking in a shower.

Tracy K. Ross, LCSW, a couples and family therapist states: "Research shows us that a relationship that's not given attention will only get worse." She adds, "If you sit back and do nothing, the relationship will deteriorate— you'll just be co-parents arguing about tasks. You have to put work into it for it to remain the same, and work even harder to improve it." (Mauer, 2019)

Below, I have listed some ways your relationship can change. These are not meant to overwhelm you. Just be mindful of them, and tuck them into your "what to watch for" pocket.

1. **Communication is all business**—It may be awhile before you are having intimate conversations across a candlelit table. For now, you may notice that you are more like passing zombies in the hallway, taking turns sleeping.

Your chatter may sound more like demands, asking for diapers or a clean blanket. This is normal for those first few weeks. After that, start being intentional with your time spent together alone without a baby. Even an hour together having conversations, not about parenting, will be exactly what you both need.

2. **Who remembers sex?**—Your sex life will change. Your body has just been through a great deal. If you adopted or had a surrogate, you too have been through an exhaustive and emotional journey. Sex is going to be the last thing new parents think about in those first few weeks. Sleep deprived, and getting the hang of this new baby thing has both of you askew. The best way to stay connected is communication. Hold each other and continue to talk about love, pleasure, and intimacy. Your sexual desire will return, all is not lost forever!

3. **Missing the spontaneity of your old life**—I hate to be the bearer of bad news, but this one is pretty much impossible until your newborn is much older. Those moments at midnight of jumping in the car for a road trip, or a last-minute weekend away with the boys. Spontaneity keeps relationships fresh and exciting, so it may be time to get creative. Because planning an outing with a newborn can feel like preparing for the

apocalypse, why not plan a movie night in the backyard under the stars? Have a conversation with your partner and discuss how important it is for both of you to plan these small dates.

4. **I need a spa day**—Couple time is important, but having "me" time makes you a better partner. After becoming a parent, that alone time is gone. Have a conversation with your partner and ask each other, "How will we maintain our self-care?" Maintaining that time you need to relax and refuel will help you be a better parent and partner.

## *Your Relationship Should Be Number One*

This sounds easy enough, doesn't it? Couples get this one wrong far more often than you would think. Once a couple becomes a family, mothers especially can be heard saying things like, "My children come first." Yes, that instinct to love and protect your children is strong, but putting their needs first is actually incorrect. I heard you gasp. Hear me out. Those precious little humans need us for absolutely everything. As they grow, they will learn life skills far beyond what we can acknowledge. They will mirror how we manage money, solve relationship issues, and even how we clean our homes. Those sponges we call our children need us. If we neglect ourselves, or our relationships because we put all our focus on them, what are they going to learn? They will have no example of self-care, mutual respect for your partner, or how a loving relationship functions.

Keeping your needs first, your mental health in check, as well as your physical health is imperative. Next in line is your relationship. That solid foundation is where you will draw strength and love from when you need it. Those precious wee humans will have the best example, watching both of you struggle, but being there for one another when it counts.

Lastly, let's not forget that your children will grow and eventually leave. I know it is hard to envision that now, but it will happen. When it does, you want to have that strong bond with your partner. If you spend all of those years focused solely on your children, what will be left to build on when they leave?

**Make Your Couple Time Count**

It is true, your couple time will be fewer and farther between now that the baby has arrived. It won't be as easy as it was to plan dates, vacations, or sporadic events. Now is the time to instill the "quality over quantity" mindset. Planning will be your best friend now, as you will have to arrange for child-care and such, but it is not impossible. The spontaneity factor will be harder to achieve, but romantic drives at midnight to soothe a crying baby can be okay for right now. It won't be easy those first few times you leave the baby and head out on the town. Resist the urge to continuously check up on the baby, once or twice is fine, but then put your focus back on the two of you. Remember, your relationship needs just as much attention as a baby.

Pro-tip, date nights don't have to be outside of the home. Once you get that wee one's schedule down pat, get them down for the night and create a romantic candlelit dinner for two with their favorite food. Too tired? Order in, throw on your jammies and a great movie. It is just the time together that counts.

## Rely on Your Spouse

This is the time you need to come together. The middle of the night feedings, the 2:00 a.m. trips to the store for more diapers, and the emotional support you will both need. It is never easy to explain the amount of physical and emotional support that will be required when a new baby comes home. New moms can begin to think they need to do it all, or else they are not maternal enough. The "mom guilt" kicks in and they may start shaming themselves.

The beautiful new bundle has two parents. They are loved and supported by two parents. Allow them to feel the bond and support from the other parent too. Just as important, you need that extra love and support. It is vital that you communicate your needs. If you are breastfeeding, ask your partner to bring the baby to you, allowing you time to get into a comfortable position. If you are still healing and need help washing your hair, or showering, ask your partner. A relaxing massage, a cup of tea, a light snack, anything to help you heal, relax, and focus on the baby, you should be asking your partner.

# Your Physical Recovery

It is understandable when a newborn enters the world, that all the focus is on them. Your health and recovery needs to be just as important. Giving your body the time and attention it needs is crucial in helping you regain strength and energy. If you put all of your focus on your new baby, and don't allow time for proper healing, you put yourself at risk for infection or injury. You want to be at your best in order to care for that precious bundle. You want to be mindful of your own body, in order to return to your healthy self. It is so easy to lose that focus due to the exhaustion and excitement of becoming a new parent.

Use those first few days to rest, relax, and refuel. Limit those visitors and don't stress about cleaning or laundry, those are all things that can wait. Be sure to have a lot of healthy meals and snacks on hand to help refuel. This time is just for bonding and healing.

The physical changes that occur in our body once we arrive home are seldom discussed. Women are often shocked and panicked to have these things happen and this should never be the case. We need to start educating and empowering women about their bodies, and the changes that occur after giving birth. I have listed some below, not to frighten you, but to educate and empower you.

1. **Who Turned On The Sweat Shower?**—A percentage of women report extreme sweating. The need to change their clothing and/or bedding. This is typically caused by your body doing its best to get rid of extra fluid and estrogen levels during postpartum. The good news is, it won't last forever. To ease the dripping, do your best to relax with some meditation, and suck back some ice water to stave off dehydration.

2. **Holy Pain Batman**—Everyone is quick to tell you how much giving birth will hurt. Nobody discusses the painful healing journey. You will hear mystical tales of women who had a vagina that whispered a baby out, climbed onto their horse and rode off into the sunset. Beautiful, and not the norm. Many things come into play, whether you had a vaginal birth, a C-section, how long the birth was, if it was natural, you get the picture. Once you get home and those "feel good" hormones and adrenaline wear off, you are going to feel as though a truck hit you. You used so many muscles to bring that body into the world. If your vagina suffered a tear, or you are now a part of the episiotomy club, I highly recommend seeing a Physical Therapist who has a speciality in pelvic floor health. They will give you exercises specific to your pelvic floor to help decrease swelling and promote circulation. Be prepared, as most doctors will tell you, the pain

will subside by six weeks. Depending on your situation, pain and swelling can last much longer than this.

3. **Bad Hair Day**—Do you think if we told moms-to-be about the hair loss, they may opt to not have children? Okay, so here is the skinny on hair and hormones. While you are pregnant, your hormones are having a party. Estrogen and progesterone are on the rise, which explains why some women go from curly to straight hair, and back again. Notice that you're losing hair? Well, once we give birth, we have a dive in those hormones, and alas, hair loss ensues. If you are choosing to breastfeed, this also has our hormones doing a dance. All of these bad postpartum hair days should be temporary, so if you find it is persisting, reach out to your healthcare team.

4. **Engorgement Woes**—Knowing that breast is best is one thing, but there are times the mom won't be able to breastfeed. Often, mama bears will not receive any information on what to expect from her breasts. So, what is engorgement? Your boobs are going to fill with milk by about day four and they are going to become hard to the touch, and very painful, and swollen. This lasts for approximately ten days after delivery. Don't be surprised to feel all over body aches, and even

a fever. A well-fitting bra will be your best friend. Keeping your breasts supported will help ease some of that pain. Ice packs will be next in line. They will help with the swelling. You will want to consider some ibuprofen or acetaminophen for the fever and to help reduce the pain.

5. **So Much Blood**—To this day, I am shocked at how many pregnant women do not know they will bleed for up to six weeks after giving birth. When they find out, their mouths almost hit the floor. How is this important piece of information still being missed? Partners are seen in the aisles of stores, middle of the night, trying to determine what maxi-pads to buy. Women are not prepared, and they need to be. You are handed a new life while they are doing god knows what below and before you know it; you are fitted with a mattress type pad, and yet still no mention of what to expect for the next SIX weeks. Women across the world will attempt their first shower at home and immediately panic at the blood clots falling from them. Screams have been heard, and phone calls to mothers have been made. This is all normal. As long as those blood clots aren't too large, you will need a large amount of maxi pads and hang on tight because this will be the longest period of your life. But hey, look at that adorable wee human you made.

## Why Should You See a Pelvic Floor Physical Therapist

We need to educate women and parents more on the gifts that pelvic floor physical therapists offer. Keep in mind all of the changes your body goes through during pregnancy. Nine months later, you put your pelvic floor through actual trauma to deliver the baby. Bringing a skilled pelvic floor health specialist even *before* your pregnancy will benefit you in ways most don't even think of.

Think of it this way, when you begin thinking about starting a family, you research everything you need to know about babies, parenthood, and even car seats. We need to educate ourselves about the toll it will take on our bodies. Our pelvis health is one area we should be investing in, as it plays a role in so much. Bad pelvis health can lead to neck and back pain, bad posture, and even infertility.

There are some fantastic benefits to seeing a Pelvic Floor Physical Therapist all through your pregnancy. I have laid out an easy-to-follow list below.

### Physical Exercise

- postural exercise
- proper breathing techniques during exercise
- pregnancy-safe exercises

## Pain

- solutions and treatment for postural pain
- pelvic pain treatment
- pregnancy treatment of hip and low back pain
- labor treatment of hip and low back pain

## Preventative

- posture and lifting while pregnant
- mindful lifting with extra front weight
- how to get up from sitting position
- proper lifting of a toddler while pregnant
- comfortable sleeping positions while pregnant
- a Pelvic Floor Physical Therapist can help
- diastasis recti (abdominal separation) prevention and treatment
- pelvic floor health and strengthening

## Preparation For Labor

- Our previous discussion about recovery times for perineum tears and episiotomies comes into play here too. Your Pelvic Floor Physical Therapist can teach you everything you need to know about perineum stretching.
- Having as many tools in your labor and delivery kit will empower you. Your pelvic floor specialist can give you amazing insight into pelvic floor relaxation strategies.
- Explore a world of birthing positions you may not have considered. Let your pelvic floor specialist

guide you into what is comfortable and works
best for you.

Adding this specialist to your healthcare team will not
only serve you well during pregnancy, but should be
considered a permanent part of the team. Below you will
see how vital they can be when you are ready to begin
exercising again.

## When Is It Safe to Exercise Again?

Getting back to a normal exercise routine is important for
your physical and mental health. It is always easiest to
start with focusing on you and baby. If it is winter, and
you are located in a colder part of the world, bundling
baby up and going for a nice walk around the block will
be great for you both. Getting out of the house and into
some fresh air will have you both in better spirits. Don't
forget to include your partner in this as well, they have
been working overtime, keeping the house together and
supporting both you and baby. If the weather is too
harsh, head over to the mall or a nice walking track at
your nearby gym or arena. A change of scenery is what
we are looking for here. Set those expectations at a
reasonable level here. If you can only walk for five or ten
minutes because you are still recovering, that is longer
than yesterday and celebrate that. Our intention here is to
increase mental and physical well-being, not make it a
negative experience. As long as you are mindful of those
expectations, you should be in a good space.

If you were one that was very active in the gym or yoga
studio prior to becoming a parent, and are anxious to
return to your previous routine, you do need to speak

with your healthcare team. Again, maintaining healthy expectations is important. Realizing you put your body through a great deal, growing a human and delivering one is a good place to start. Go easy, rest when your body tells you to, and hydrate often.

It is standard for doctors to clear you by six weeks postpartum for physical activity. For many, this is not long enough for your body to heal. You have to be educated as to what type of activity is safe and when. If you throw on that workout gear and head to the gym and begin doing crunches, you could do more harm than good.

Bringing that pelvic floor specialist on board during this time would be crucial. Ask them all of those questions you may have regarding your previous routines. They will know how your body is recovering and can be sure you won't be doing harm. Remember to take it slow. Your first step should just be getting outdoors, soaking up some vitamin D on a nice walk. Remember, both are great for your physical and mental health. Each time you want to ramp up to something a bit more challenging, just check in with your health care team, including your pelvic floor specialist. They will be able to monitor how your healing journey is going and if it is safe to move to the next level of exercise.

# Chapter 7:

# Magic Tips and Tricks

This is the one section of the book you will want to keep handy. As promised, it contains the best and most-proven tips and tricks from me, the author of this book. Some call me the professional baby whisperer, and I have committed my life to easing babies of their pain, tension, and discomfort. With 20 years of experience, I am a Craniosacral Therapist who believes in helping families feel at peace again.

Before you begin these secret tips, I want you to know that you do not need to understand the complex science of the body and your baby's operating system, in order to help them. You have the intention to help. That is all you need to know for these techniques. I do not expect everyone to fully "feel" with your hands what I'm asking you to do, because babies rhythms are super light, almost indecipherable but you can do them with great results. How do I know? I've given these magic tricks to HUNDREDS of parents, I've done them on THOUSANDS of patients over the span of my career and I know that you can do this! I'm cheering you on. Just keep these few things in mind to be successful.

1. Take a breath before you touch your baby.
2. Make eye contact and ask them if you can help?

3. Lighter is always better. Ask yourself if you can do this with less pressure. Every single time. A kiss of a feather is all you need.
4. Practice makes progress.

## *Magic Hand Placement aka The Baby Sandwich*

Place the baby laying on their back—the best place would be on your lap, or on the changing table.

Slide one hand under the baby's back, follow along the ribs, and lay the baby flat on top of your hand. Place your other hand on the baby's upper belly, but just kiss the ribcage. There is no pressure added to the baby other than just the weight of your hands, just stay and feel; in a few moments things start to soften, you might feel heat being released or a tiny pulse like a heartbeat under your hands. You can stay in this position for minutes–on average, two to five minutes is plenty. If you feel extra rumbles, watch the baby tighten going into the lower belly, you can move your hands down, hands supporting the sacrum (butt bone) and top hand placed below the belly button.

The technique is used to calm and reduce the tone of the vagus nerve. Remember that "stress" is what is causing "symptoms"; reducing tone will assist in learning to swallow properly (milk or food), digest food properly (without colic, reflux, or constipation), and help your baby be happy and content when not eating.

## The Dural Tube

The next trick is going to help the dural tube. The dural tube is the lining from inside the skull that ends in the sacrum coccyx. It contains cerebrospinal fluid, supplies the body, and gets vital nutrients to the brain and spinal cord. It helps circulate immune cells, neurotransmitters, and hormones. When there is imbalance, restriction, injury, or stress, the dural tube is being pulled by fascia. Fascia surrounds the dura mater and all internal organs, it is a network of connective tissue that connects all parts of the body. Fascial tissue also forms a layer around each bone, ligament, tendon, and muscle, as well as every individual muscle fiber and nerve fiber—all the way down to the cellular level. This wave technique will help release any "stickiness" from the inside of the dural tube and allow the body to "reboot."

## The Wave–The Magic Move That Makes Everything Better

A Baby's system runs so lightly it is hard to palpate, but you can mechanically do this technique without needing to "feel" for it.

To begin, visualize a lakeshore where a few waves are coming from across the water. The wave technique is going to watch a wave go out for five seconds and then come back in for five seconds. Your hands are going to facilitate the tide. Back and forth for several cycles.

To start, lay the baby on the change table or on the floor with you sitting beside them. Use two to three soft fingers under the back of the baby's head, not the neck, like you're balancing a feather on your fingers. At the same time, feel like you are supporting their head and not applying upward pressure on your baby. Next, slide your other hand under the baby's butt, use three or four fingers and just let the baby's body weight come into your hand. Count to five.

## 1. DOUBLE WAVE

Now, "feel like" you're stretching the baby in both directions, as both hands move away from each other (butt hand towards the feet, hand on the head moving further towards top of head) ever soooo slightly. This is barely a move, if you felt like you moved your hands, you can do it next time with less. Your baby will feel like they are being stretched across the room. Then, count to five, and very slowly release any pull you had in your hands. Count to five again. Repeat this double wave, one to three times.

## 2. SINGLE ALTERNATE WAVES

Only move from the butt stretching away, leaving the hand under the head totally still.

Hold for five seconds and then release.

Count to five and then the fingers under the head will move away. Count to five and release.

You MIGHT feel a very slight pulse, almost like a heartbeat. You could also feel some heat, or see the baby start to relax and with luck go still while you do this. Even if you don't feel or see, remember this is working under the surface!

## The Tongue Check

When the baby is clicking, biting, not effectively nursing or taking a bottle, if they are suffering from reflux or have gas, this little technique of "oral play" will help your baby reorganize their tongue. The tongue, like any other muscle, can get tight, tough, and lose its function; babies are learning how to use it, but when they start becoming dysfunctional, they need to relearn how to use it. Does your baby's tongue deviate to one side? Have you seen your baby stick their tongue out past their lips? If it is a yes to deviation, there is a weakness from under the tongue in the hypoglossal nerve, which helps the tongue move food in the mouth to swallow

If you haven't seen the tongue past the lips, we can wonder if the frenulum (the little piece of tissue under the tongue) is anchoring it down tightly to the floor of the mouth.

## Assess: What Is the Tongue Doing?

I divide the tongue into four sections from front to back.

Imagine point one is at the tip of the tongue, and four is at the back of the tongue. If you put your finger in the baby's mouth, the pad of your finger from tip to first knuckle will be doing the "work".

To start, break the seal on the baby if you are nursing or remove the bottle from their mouth. I then want you to put a clean finger, index, or pinky finger on top of the baby's tongue, pad side down. What happens? The baby should make a trough and pull your finger into their mouth deeply, and there should be a very solid suction, like a vacuum happening. Don't over think what you feel. If you think it feels weak, you are probably right, or if the baby is trying to do anything but suck your finger, moving tongue side to side or not at all, that is also a sign they need a little help. Notice where the baby is using the tongue from. Are they starting the motion from the front or from the back? It should be a locomotive motion from the back if they are using it without muscle restriction in the under tongue muscles called the supra hyoid muscles whose role it is to help open the mouth, and facilitate swallowing.

## Lion's Breath

Place your finger, pad side down, on the tongue in what I say is position one to three, on the tongue and just "pretend" you have Velcro attaching your finger to the tongue. I want you to "feel like" you are bringing the tongue forward out of the mouth using a minimal amount of traction towards the lips. This is a stretch that opens space at the back of the tongue as it moves down into the esophagus. Baby might gag, or yawn just a bit when this move is done, but we know we are on the right track to letting this release. This is a baby's version of a fabulous yoga breathing practice, Lion's Breath that helps stimulate the throat and upper chest in kids and adults!

## Under the Tongue

Second, slip a finger under the tongue using the pad of your finger, move along the tongue muscle as far as you can go, without gagging the baby. Gentle touch...

Does it feel like the surface of a sticky marshmallow? A balloon? Does it feel rigid or firm? Do you feel a "speed bump"? Is it lumpy? Would you describe it as slippery, or smooth? Compare sides and just notice if one side is softer than the other.

Then with the weight of a feather, gently press inwards to the tongue muscle on the "stronger, stickier, lumpy" side. The lighter you touch, the more you will influence the fascial system. (Elim patterns live in these babies.) Always remember to do both sides.

You can try it on yourself—the majority of people hold a lot of tension in the tongue and can influence their jaw tension, TMJ, etc., from gentle touches under the tongue.

Next, turn your finger downwards into the floor of the mouth GENTLY. Does it rebound right back like pressing into a balloon? Or does it sink into the tissue like a melting marshmallow?

We want it to soften from a firm state into a soft, gooey state, so start at the back where the molars would be down in the floor of the mouth. Very slowly, with a feather- light "sweep" from the back towards the front, and repeat x2. For areas of tension, you can add a finger from the other hand under the chin and follow the inside finger like a magnet. Repeat x2 each side.

After your last sweep, take your finger out of the baby's mouth for a minute, so things can soften and allow a "reboot" to take place. Then, you're going to recheck the trough and suck. Did it improve? Just notice what the baby is doing or not doing. Go back to feeding the baby and remember LESS is often MORE. These are muscles that can bruise if touch is too much, they will be tender for the baby as they are retraining, but I encourage you to do this for a few days with every feed and then taper as needed. Remember to be gentle as a feather, and ask yourself if you can do it with less, and your finger will follow!

Before we depart the world of tongues, I wanted to leave you with a fun game to play with your wee one. While they are facing you and you have their attention, stick your tongue out at them. Yes, you heard me right. Keep doing this and see if they will stick their wee tongue back out at you. This is one of the first ways to teach them about communicating with people. Slowly, they are realizing that they can respond to someone, and if they patiently wait their turn, people will respond back. You are helping your baby learn how to communicate before they can even speak!

# Conclusion

I set out to create a book that was unlike most. It had to cover pregnancy, childbirth, recovery, and parenting. More than that, I wanted to encompass all of the family dynamics while being inclusive of any parental unit.

It was important that this book was real, raw, and honest. It is easy to research anything in today's world. Because of that, parents are searching for more, searching for better ways to treat their newborns. No longer are they sitting back and taking outdated medical research as the only answer. Having the ability to provide alternate options for not only the care of the baby, but the physical and mental care of both parents was a priority when writing this book.

I hope that by giving you alternatives, you can know you have choices. Education and knowledge are powerful resources, and it is okay to continue to learn about these wonderful options available to you.

Becoming parents can feel euphoric and guilt-ridden all at the same time, but it doesn't have to. Generations before us leaned in for help. Family, neighbors, and good friends would surround a new family with meals, baby care and mama care, without being asked. Today, we are isolating ourselves and have adapted a superhuman mentality. We bring baby home, and by day two, we feel pressure to post photos of a sparkling clean home, baby adorned in a tutu, cute saying on their onesie, and the obligatory hashtag, #parentingwin, #lovinglife, or #momboss. It likely took you eight hours just to get that perfect shot, the baby probably threw up on four outfits, and you refused to even be in the photo. You have likely received some text messages with offers of help, and you nicely replied that you are fine, despite wanting a warm meal and some laundry done. There is just no way we can appear as if we don't have our shit together. That is a weakness. You are not weak, humanity is just a bit off at the moment.

Our healthcare systems across the world are changing. You need to be the captain of your wellness ship. Once you begin, you will feel empowered while you build your healthcare team. Listen to what your body needs, it will tell you. Build your team around the needs of your family and live the healthiest, best life you can.

I want this book to reiterate the truth. Parenthood is messy and amazing. Newborns are precious and poop factories. Giving birth is a miracle and the healing is more painful than most will tell you. Doctor's should not be the only people on your healthcare team.

I have listed some great Instagram pages to follow below. I have included them because they hold many of the same beliefs as covered in this book. Natural, safe, and educated care for families and children. They can be a great resource for you, as you move through your parenting journey.

@KydKydro                  @snooze.clues

@grassrootshw              @progressthroughplay

@Luxfamilychiro            @Infant.feeding.specialist

@tonguetiebabies           @kindredchiropracticnz

@beardfamiliychiropractic

# About the Author

**Becky Brezovski**

Meet Becky Brezovski, the professional baby whisperer. She has earned this title not only through extensive education but also through her multiple years of treating and soothing babies and their families.

A Registered Massage Therapist, and a Craniosacral Therapist with advanced training in pediatric care from NICU babies—premature, into adolescence. She sees 250 infants in her clinic per year. On average, 10-20 children walk through her doors per week, from baby through to adolescence. The main issues she sees infants for are birth trauma, tongue tie, sleep, reflux, sensory processing disorders, neuro integrations, motor delays etc., and all of these are tied back to the birth.

But wait, there's more! From the treatment table to the yoga mat, Becky has also been a trained yoga instructor for over twenty years. She finds joy in teaching both families and children how to find calm and inner peace within their bodies. With her education, training, and life skills, she is able to offer a complete package of healing and wellness.

Becky's clinical practice is unique and in high demand. Families drive from hours away to seek her advice and treatment. Becky's expertise is clinical, she has 20 years of experience to back up her advice. Her mantra is "when you heal the baby, you heal the whole family."

# Glossary

- **Adult Bedtime Stories**: That 30 minutes you take for yourself before bed to catch up on all your Instagram stories.

- **Blowouts**: High-pressure poop spray. Yes, you read that correctly. Not to be confused with toots, or poo's, this situation will have you ducking for cover. Don't stress too much, once your wee one begins solid foods, these poo showers should be a thing of the past.

- **Booger Sucker**: Picture a turkey baster, but a smaller version that can fit in your hand. Now, this is going to be placed, oh so gently, at the base of your baby's nostril and used to suck the snot out of their nose. I can't make this sh*t up!

- **Butt Paste**: Thick as wallpaper paste, and comes in many forms, this will be a godsend for you. A nice thick layer of bum cream to ward off diaper rash.

- **Carcolepsy**: That child you have that refuses to sleep or nap, keeping you awake for days at a time, but the minute you put them in the car and start the engine…OUT COLD.

- **Crap Cradle**: The baby bouncer/jolly jumper that you plop the baby into because you know all they need is some movement to get those bowels moving.

- **Dad Spa**: The glorious steam facial and sauna one receives as he graciously unloads the dishwasher.
- **Date Night**: When you finally feel confident enough to leave the baby with your parents or a friend to get dressed up and hit the town with your partner. You are then exhausted after your shower, so you order in, drink some wine, and fall asleep on the couch by 8:30 p.m.
- **Deja Poo**: Bringing a baby home is an invitation to poop, a lot of poop. Deja poo occurs when you have changed five poopy diapers, and you just finished changing one, when you immediately smell poop again. You begin doubting your sanity…did I not just change a poop filled surprise? Welcome to deja poo.
- **Dream Feeding**: No, this is not the ability to eat whatever you dream of. It is the art of feeding your wee human whilst they are on the brink of sleeping in hopes of them sleeping longer.
- **Freezer Tapas**: Digging to the bottom of that freezer to serve up the family a gourmet dinner of fish sticks and two-year-old french fries. You're welcome.
- **Going to Bed Early!**: We all know getting to bed early after bringing home a newborn is next to impossible. So what is this code for? Sex! Yep, friends want to visit, or the mother-in-law was

going to bring over a casserole, well dang-it, we were just heading to bed early (sorry not sorry).

- **Lawnmower Parent**: We have all heard of helicopter parenting, but this one is far more aggressive. They will actually "mow" down anything and everything in their child's way to assure they succeed.

- **Mombie**: Part Mom, part zombie, next level exhaustion. Colicky baby? Teething baby? Makes no difference, if you are that mom who is now running on .5 hours of sleep, welcome to the Mombie Club.

- **Mom Bun**: The act of coiling your luscious locks upon your head to avoid the likes of baby vomit, poop, and even your morning coffee.

- **Nepootism**: I did not think it was possible, but it is. You will actually get to know the smell of your own baby's poop. "Sniff sniff, oh yep, that one is mine."

- **Nipple Confusion**: No, your baby is not confused about "what" a nipple is. They do know this is where my food comes from. What can happen—they can be confused about "why" they cannot suck the same and develop bad habits when introduced to bottles and pacifiers which in turn makes feeding harder.

- **Nipple Shields**: Visions of armor placed gallantly across one's chest to protect said nipples from battle, but no. These silicone beauties go over your natural nipple, acting as a second "extended" nipple for preemies who have difficulty latching, or babies with tongue ties too.

- **Parental Full Night's Sleep**: Five hours, for the next 18 years.
- **Peepee Teepee**: Clearly, a few too many parents were getting sprayed in the face by their baby boys urine stream during diaper changes. This invention is a cotton, reusable, and washable "penis tent" you place over their pee pee, to prevent being peed on again. Trust me, over time you will instinctively use your hand, and become super fast at swapping out those diapers.
- **Poonami**: A level ten poo explosion requiring all hands on deck, I repeat all hands on deck. This is the highest of all poo explosion levels, we never know if the clothing or parental unit will survive this one.
- **Road Trip**: Just doesn't carry the same meaning as it did in your college years. Now, it is buckling that crying baby into the car and aimlessly driving around in hopes they will nap.
- **Russian Poo-lette**: We have all done it. We smell the poo, but we are in complete denial that the poo has occurred. So, what do we do next? We shove our fingers down the back of the diaper and are oftentimes met with, well you get the gist.
- **The Milk Truck**: If your baby mama is breast feeding, we highly suggest leaving this slang term

to others when referring to her. Maybe you could try the warmer version of breast buffet?

- **Toilet Biscuits**: Any and all treats that you have no choice but to eat while hiding in the bathroom. This is necessary so as not to have to share with children, or to just have a moment to yourself. We don't judge, eat the biscuits.
- **Spinach**: Any decadent, savory, or delicious snack, or meal that you are enjoying and absolutely refuse to share with your child.

# References

Athena, S. (2020, March 1). *Sleep and brain development: An important connection.* Nested Bean. https://www.nestedbean.com/blogs/zen-blog/sleep-brain-development-for-babies

Aziz, S. (2022, June 4). *Babies of COVID-19: The impact of being born during the pandemic.* Global News. https://globalnews.ca/news/8890300/canada-covid-pandemic-babies/

*Baby cues and baby body language: a guide.* (2022, March 14). Raising Children Network. https://raisingchildren.net.au/newborns/connecting-communicating/communicating/baby-cues

Berk, S. (2020, May 6). *The Benefits of Tummy Time.* Parents. https://www.parents.com/baby/development/physical/the-benefits-of-tummy-time/

Bordoni B, Morabito B, Mitrano R, Simonelli M, Toccafondi A. *The Anatomical Relationships of the Tongue with the Body System.* Cureus. 2018 Dec 5;10(12):e3695. doi: 10.7759/cureus.3695. PMID: 30838167; PMCID: PMC6390887.

Cautero, R. M. (2019, March 12). *Why So Many Babies Are Getting Their Tongues Clipped.* The Atlantic. https://www.theatlantic.com/family/archive/2019/03/breast-feeding-and-tongue-tie/584503/

Chamberlain, D. (1998). *The Mind of Your Newborn Baby.*
North Atlantic Books.
https://www.amazon.ca/Mind-Your-Newborn-
Baby/dp/155643264X (Original work published
1988)

Coley, R. (2015). The Flat Head Syndrome Fix: A Parent's
Guide to Simple and Surprising Strategies for
Preventing Plagiocephaly and Rounding Out
Baby's Flat Spots Without a Helmet. *In Google
Books* (pp. 12–36). CanDo Kiddo.

*Colostrum: What Is It, Benefits & What To Expect.* (2022).
Cleveland Clinic.
**https://my.clevelandclinic.org/health/body/
22434-
colostrum#:~:text=Colostrum%20is%20the%
20first%20form**

Contributors, W. E. (2021, March 12). *What is a lip tie?*
WebMD. https://www.webmd.com/baby/what-
is-a-lip-
tie#:~:text=Dental%20Issues.&text=Lip%20ties
%20often%20lead%20to

David Barnes Chamberlain. (1998). *The mind of your
newborn baby.* North Atlantic Books.

Dewar, G. (2022, July 20). *Dream feeding: An evidence-based
guide to helping babies sleep longer.* PARENTING
SCIENCE. https://parentingscience.com/dream-
feeding/#:~:text=Dream%20feeding%20has%20
been%20defined

Dubinsky |, D. (n.d.). *Harvey Karp's "happiest baby" method
for baby sleep and soothing.* BabyCenter. Retrieved
August 27, 2022, from

https://www.babycenter.com/baby/sleep/harvey
-karps-happiest-baby-method-for-baby-sleep-and-
soothin_10373838#:~:text=Newborns%20don

Francis, G. (2019, January 21). *Top 20 "funniest" phrases
used by modern parents*. The Independent.
**https://www.independent.co.uk/life-
style/parenting-phrases-slang-funny-mums-
dads-mombie-iparenting-ginwag-mumboss-
a8738571.html**

Frey, A. (2022). *Whole body baby: A craniosacral therapy
handbook for families.*
**https://www.amazon.com/Whole-Body-
Baby-CranioSacral-Handbook-
ebook/dp/B0B86PJXGC**

Galley, J. (2018, January 8). *Parenting slang: A guide for all
modern hot mess mums* | mum central.
Mumcentral.com.au.
https://mumcentral.com.au/parenting-slang-
guide/

Geddes, D., Kent, J., & Hartmann, P. (2008). Tongue
movement and intra-oral vacuum in breastfeeding
infants. *National Library of Medicine.*
https://doi.org/10.1016

Hoffman Cullinan, D. (2016, August 16). *10 Easy Ways to
Set Yourself up for Breastfeeding Success in Life and
Work.* **https://www.momsrising.org/blog/10-
easy-ways-to-set-yourself-up-for-
breastfeeding-success-in-life-and-work**

Howland, G. (2018, April 24). *Lip tie: How to check your
baby (and how to fix it)*. Mama Natural.
https://www.mamanatural.com/lip-tie/

Kelly, K. M., Littlefield, T. R., Pomatto, J. K., Ripley, C. E., Beals, S. P., & Joganic, E. F. (1999). Importance of Early Recognition and Treatment of Deformational Plagiocephaly with Orthotic Cranioplasty. *The Cleft Palate-Craniofacial Journal*, 36(2), 127–130. https://doi.org/10.1597/1545-1569_1999_036_0127_ioerat_2.3.co_2

Larrain, M., & Stevenson, E. G. J. (2022). Controversy Over Tongue-Tie: Divisions in the Community of Healthcare Professionals. *Medical Anthropology*, 41(4), 446–459. https://doi.org/10.1080/01459740.2022.2056843

Mauer et al. 2019 *Psychoanalytic Work with Families and Couples: Clinical Perspectives on Suffering (1st ed.)*. Routledge. **http://doi.org/10.4324/9780429316241**

Mayo Clinic. (2018, September 1). *Postpartum depression - Symptoms and Causes*. Mayo Clinic. https://www.mayoclinic.org/diseases-conditions/postpartum-depression/symptoms-causes/syc-20376617

McCarthy, K. (2022). *40+ Funny New Baby Quotes to Make Anyone Laugh Out Loud*. LoveToKnow. https://baby.lovetoknow.com/newborn/40-funny-new-baby-quotes-make-anyone-laugh-out-loud

*Merriam-Webster Dictionary*. (2022). Merriam-Webster.com. https://www.merriam-webster.com/dictionary/postpartum%20depression?utm_campaign=sd&utm_medium=serp&utm_source=jsonld

Newman, S. (2017, December 14). Study Underscores *Why Fewer Toys Is the Better Option* | Psychology Today. Www.psychologytoday.com. https://www.psychologytoday.com/us/blog/sing letons/201712/study-underscores-why-fewer-toys-is-the-better-option

O'Connor NR, Tanabe KO, Siadaty MS, Hauck FR. *Pacifiers and breastfeeding: a systematic review.* Arch Pediatr Adolesc Med. 2009 Apr;163(4):378-82. doi: 10.1001/archpediatrics.2008.578. PMID: 19349568.

Pacheco, D., & Singh, Dr. A. (2022, March 11). *Infant Sleep Cycles: How Are They Different From Adults?* Sleep Foundation; OneCare Media. **https://www.sleepfoundation.org/baby-sleep/baby-sleep-cycle**

Packham, A. (2017, April 4). *New parenting slang: Do you know the meaning of these 20 phrases?* HuffPost UK. https://www.huffingtonpost.co.uk/entry/new-parenting-slang-words-list_uk_58e367cbe4b03a26a365a93f

*The importance of touch.* (2016, October 10). The Developmental Baby Massage Centre. **http://www.thebabieswebsite.com/the-importance-of-touch/**

The Mama Coach (2020, April 24). *How Do I Prevent My Baby From Developing a Flat Head?* - The Mama Coach. The Mama Coach. **https://themamacoach.com/how-do-i-prevent-my-baby-from-developing-a-flat-head/**

Thompson, R. (2012, March 26). *Book I: Consciously Parenting. The Consciously Parenting Project.* https://consciouslyparenting.com/consciously-parenting/

*What Is Conscious Parenting? Key Points, Benefits, and Drawbacks.* (2020, April 24). Healthline. **https://www.healthline.com/health/parenting/conscious-parenting#benefits**

# Image References

Crave, F. (2015). *Baby mother infant child* [Online Image]. In pixabay.com. **https://pixabay.com/photos/baby-mother-infant-child-female-821625/**

Man woman dog pet pug owners. (2017). [Online Image]. *In pixabay.com.* https://pixabay.com/photos/man-woman-dog-pet-pug-owners-2425121/

Pictures, P. D. (2012). *Father baby portrait* [Online Image]. In pixabay.com. **https://pixabay.com/photos/father-baby-portrait-infant-22194/**

Prudente, P. (2017). *Cesarean birth* [Online]. In Unsplash. https://unsplash.com/photos/-P2djqAwM8U

Sampaio, L. (2020). *Breastfeeding baby* [Online Image]. In pixabay.com. **https://pixabay.com/photos/breastfeeding-breastfeeding-baby-5477488/**

Studios, P. (2021). *Cute little infant child lying on his belly on bed at home* [Online Image]. In Istockphoto.com. https://www.istockphoto.com/photo/cute-little-infant-child-lying-on-his-belly-on-bed-at-home-gm1331245251-414437388